B1 Preliminary test content in *Own It!* Level 3 has been checked by Cambridge Assessment English for accuracy and level.

WORKBOOK

Annie Cornford and Andrew Reid

CAMBRIDGE
UNIVERSITY PRESS

University Printing House, Cambridge CB2 8BS, United Kingdom

One Liberty Plaza, 20th Floor, New York, NY 10006, USA

477 Williamstown Road, Port Melbourne, VIC 3207, Australia

314–321, 3rd Floor, Plot 3, Splendor Forum, Jasola District Centre, New Delhi – 110025, India

79 Anson Road, #06–04/06, Singapore 079906

José Abascal, 56–10, 28003 Madrid, Spain

Cambridge University Press is part of the University of Cambridge.

It furthers the University's mission by disseminating knowledge in the pursuit of education, learning and research at the highest international levels of excellence.

www.cambridge.org
Information on this title: www.cambridge.org/978-1-108-71481-5

© Cambridge University Press 2020

This publication is in copyright. Subject to statutory exception and to the provisions of relevant collective licensing agreements, no reproduction of any part may take place without the written permission of Cambridge University Press.

First published 2020

20 19 18 17 16 15 14 13 12 11 10 9 8 7 6 5 4 3 2 1

Printed in Dubai by Oriental Press

A catalogue record for this publication is available from the British Library

ISBN 978-1-108-71481-5 Own it Workbook Level 3

ISBN 978-84-9036-855-8 Collaborate Workbook Level 3

Additional resources for this publication at www. cambridge.org/ownit/resources

Cambridge University Press has no responsibility for the persistence or accuracy of URLs for external or third-party internet websites referred to in this publication, and does not guarantee that any content on such websites is, or will remain, accurate or appropriate. Information regarding prices, travel timetables, and other factual information given in this work is correct at the time of first printing but Cambridge University Press does not guarantee the accuracy of such information thereafter.

CONTENTS

Starter Unit	Welcome!	p4
Unit 1	Be inspired	p8
Unit 2	What is art?	p16
Unit 3	Spread the word!	p24
Unit 4	Healthy body, healthy mind	p32
Unit 5	Save our planet!	p40
Unit 6	Think outside the box	p48
Unit 7	A world of celebration	p56
Unit 8	Back to school	p64
Unit 9	A holiday on the moon	p72

Exam tips and practice	p80
Language reference and practice	p86
Language Bank	p106
Irregular Verbs	p111

STARTER

VOCABULARY AND READING
Technology

1 ⭐ **Complete the sentences with the words in the box.**

> apps ~~devices~~ emoji message
> screen social media

1 My grandparents haven't got many electronic ___devices___.
2 Do your eyes get tired when you look at the computer _____ for a long time?
3 We learn a lot about famous people by following them on _____.
4 Bella sends her mum a text _____ when she's late home.
5 My favourite _____ are Snapchat and BuzzFeed.
6 Which emotions can't you express with an _____?

Feelings

2 ⭐⭐ **Circle the correct words.**
1 Mason gets (embarrassed) / excited when his mum puts his baby photos on *Facebook*.
2 I'm getting *tired* / *excited* about tonight's party!
3 You always do well in exams so don't be *nervous* / *bored*.
4 Janek was so *embarrassed* / *tired* that he fell asleep at his desk.
5 Mandy's crying – what's she *upset* / *excited* about?
6 We're always so busy that we haven't got time to get *tired* / *bored*.

3 ⭐⭐⭐ **Write an example sentence for the words below.**
1 embarrassed _____
2 app _____
3 screen _____

A message on an app

4 ⭐ **Read the conversation. How are Louise and Yanis spending the summer?**
_____

YANIS	Hey! How's the filmmaking course? Are you enjoying it?
LOUISE	It's great, thanks. And you? I hope you're not getting bored.
YANIS	I hardly ever get bored – I love getting new ideas and dancing in front of the group.
LOUISE	Don't you sometimes feel embarrassed?
YANIS	Not at all! But I'm new to street dance, so I often get upset if I forget the steps. What kind of films are you making?
LOUISE	We're not making a whole film until the end of the course. I'm so excited about that!
YANIS	So what do they teach you?
LOUISE	We're learning to use different devices like video cameras and music apps.
YANIS	Cool!
LOUISE	After lunch we usually write film scripts or practise doing make-up or costumes.
YANIS	They're making a short video of our final show – I'm a bit nervous about that!
LOUISE	Why? You're a great dancer! Hey, maybe I can make a film about you one day!

5 ⭐⭐⭐ **Answer the questions.**
1 How does Yanis show that he is confident?
_____
2 When does Yanis sometimes feel unhappy?
_____
3 What is Louise excited about?
_____
4 What idea does Louise have for a film?
_____

LANGUAGE IN ACTION AND VOCABULARY

Present simple and present continuous with adverbs of frequency

1 ★ Put the words in the correct order to make sentences.

1 ever / upset / gets / He / hardly /
   He hardly ever gets upset.
2 steps / remember / I / the / don't / always
   _____
3 embarrassed / dance / often / Do / when / get / you / you / ?
   _____
4 music / the / films / We / for / write / the / sometimes
   _____
5 him / His / never / teachers / angry / get / with
   _____

2 ★★ Circle the correct words.

1 She *'s playing* / *plays* a computer game now.
2 I *often feel* / *'m often feeling* bored at home.
3 *Does Mario sometimes send* / *Is Mario sometimes sending* you photos?
4 The course is great: I *'m having* / *have* a great time.
5 I *usually text* / *'m usually texting* my friend when I can't do my homework.

Present simple for future

3 ★★ Write questions and answers about the future.

1 What time / the lesson begin tomorrow ? / at nine
   What time does the lesson begin tomorrow?
   It begins at nine.
2 When / Tom arrive in Japan ? / tomorrow morning
   _____
3 What day / we get the exam results ? / on Friday
   _____
4 When / your music lesson finish? / at midday
   _____

Music

4 ★ Circle nine more music words in the sound wave.

heavymetalfolkdrumsreggaejazzfansbassDJrapkeyboard

5 ★★ Match the definitions with words from Exercise 4.

1 a loud, round instrument you play with your hands or sticks drums
2 a person who plays music and talks on the radio or at a club _____
3 music popular in Jamaica with a strong rhythm _____
4 an electric instrument similar to a guitar with low notes _____
5 music and songs in a traditional style _____
6 an electronic instrument similar to a piano _____
7 the artist usually speaks the words in this type of music _____
8 people who love a band or musician _____

6 ★★ Complete the advert with the words in the box.

DJ   drums   ~~fan~~   heavy metal   jazz   rap

Are you a big ¹ fan of music? Do you sing like a bird or is ² _____ more your thing (fan of Tinie Tempah maybe?). Do you play a musical instrument like the guitar, bass or ³ _____ ? Or perhaps you want to be a ⁴ _____ because you prefer to play records, not an instrument? From relaxing, easy-listening ⁵ _____ to fast, loud ⁶ _____ , you can learn and practise it all at MLA Music Summer Camp. Click on the link below for more information!

MORE INFO

LISTENING AND LANGUAGE IN ACTION
A conversation

1 ★ Look at the photo. Where are the people?

_____

2 ★ Listen to the conversation. Why does Maria go to the event in Exercise 1 every year?

_____

3 ★★ Listen again. Are the sentences T (true) or F (false)?
1 The organisers of MusicFest sell the tickets in a lottery. __T__
2 Maria doesn't pay for her ticket. ____
3 She works every evening. ____
4 Maria hears and sees all the bands. ____
5 She loves the music, but doesn't like the hot weather. ____

4 ★★★ Listen again. Why do Maria and Noel mention the words in the box?

excited   fans   reggae singers   tired

excited: Noel says Maria looks excited.
_____
_____
_____

Past simple

5 ★ Complete the sentences with the past simple form of the verbs in brackets.
1 Ela _wrote_ (write) a great song and _____ (sing) it for us last night.
2 We _____ (take) the dogs and _____ (go) for a long walk on the beach.
3 I _____ (know) you were here because I _____ (see) your coat.
4 _____ she _____ (make) a CD for Luca's birthday?
5 Marcus _____ (not tell) us that he _____ (have) concert tickets for all of us.

6 ★★ Complete the sentences with the correct past simple form of the verbs in the box.

be (x2)   learn   not enjoy   ~~play~~
fall   work

1 The heavy metal band _played_ really loud music.
2 We _____ the words to all the new songs.
3 The students _____ very hard before their exam.
4 Joe _____ embarrassed when he _____ on the ice.
5 I _____ the concert last night. It _____ boring.

7 ★★★ Write questions about Maria and MusicFest from Exercise 2. Then write the correct answers.
1 the organisers of MusicFest / sent Maria a letter / ?
Did the organisers of MusicFest send Maria a letter?
No, they didn't. They sent her an email.
2 Maria / ask the organisers for a free ticket / ?
_____
_____
3 Maria / get a ticket in the lottery / ?
_____
_____
4 Maria / work at the campsite in the evening last year / ?
_____
_____
5 it / rain all weekend at MusicFest last year / ?
_____
_____

WRITING
A review of an app

1 ⭐ Look at the advert. What do you think the app does? _____

WordFind — Great for every English language learner!

2 ⭐⭐ Read Ben's review and check your answer to Exercise 1.

A WordFind is a great app for English language learners, especially when you are studying alone. Our teacher told us about it in class. He said he uses it all the time, so I decided to try it. Last week I downloaded it on my phone and I love it!

B It's good because the definitions are very easy to understand. It tells you what each word means in simple English, and how and when you can use it. You can also search for a word by saying it. I can't always find a word I'm looking for when I don't know how to spell it, so this is very useful.

C In my opinion, there are a couple of problems with it. It tells you where each word comes from and when people first used it, but I'm not interested in the history of words. Also, it's expensive – there are lots of free dictionary apps, though maybe they're not as good.

D Overall, I think WordFind is a great app because you can use it anywhere and it's easy to use. I would definitely recommend it.

3 ⭐⭐ Which paragraph (A–D) …
1 explains the bad things about the app? __C__
2 gives Ben's general opinion? _____
3 introduces the app? _____
4 explains the good things about the app? _____

4 ⭐⭐ Complete the *Useful language* phrases with the words in the box.

> great   ~~language~~   opinion   Overall   problems   recommend

1 WordFind is a _language_-learning app.
2 It's _____ because you can use it anywhere.
3 I would definitely _____ it to all English language learners.
4 _____, I think it's a great app.
5 In my _____, there are a couple of _____ with it.

Write your own review of a language-learning app.

PLAN
5 ⭐⭐ Write notes about an app you use.

What is it? _____

What's good about it? _____

What isn't good about it? _____

What's your general opinion? _____

6 Decide what information to include in each paragraph. Use the information in Exercise 3 to help you.

WRITE
7 ⭐⭐⭐ Write your review. Remember to include four paragraphs, the present simple and present continuous, adverbs of frequency, and phrases from the *Useful language* box (see Student's Book, p9).

CHECK
8 Do you …
- introduce the app in the first paragraph?
- write about good and bad things?
- give your general opinion?

1 BE INSPIRED

VOCABULARY
Describing people

1 ⭐ Find 11 more personality adjectives in the word search.

A	M	C	O	N	F	I	D	E	N	T	R
M	S	A	F	D	A	S	E	G	R	E	G
B	S	L	F	E	Y	C	U	Z	J	X	I
I	E	M	I	D	T	N	V	K	C	S	N
T	P	R	O	F	E	N	T	U	H	O	S
I	A	O	B	A	E	D	C	N	E	C	P
O	T	R	S	C	S	S	E	D	E	I	I
U	I	A	C	T	O	N	F	F	R	A	R
S	E	N	S	I	T	I	V	E	F	B	I
G	N	B	E	V	R	Y	W	B	U	L	N
F	T	R	S	E	N	S	I	B	L	E	G
N	G	H	E	L	P	F	U	L	J	W	B
T	A	L	E	N	T	E	D	B	N	Y	S

2 ⭐⭐ Complete the sentences with words from Exercise 1.

1 People think I'm __confident__, but I'm usually shy.
2 Paul isn't very _____. He likes being alone.
3 Tyler is usually very _____. He's always smiling.
4 Kim and her brother are very different. He's silly and immature, but she's _____.
5 It's better to be _____ and not panic in dangerous situations.
6 I'm very _____ – I get upset easily.

3 ⭐⭐ Complete the table with the opposites of words from Exercise 1.

in-	¹ sensitive	im-	⁷ _____
un-	² _____		
	³ _____		
	⁴ _____		
	⁵ _____		
	⁶ _____		

4 ⭐⭐ Complete the sentences with the opposites in the box.

| ~~anxious~~ grumpy lazy shy silly |

1 Martin isn't calm today. He's __anxious__ because of his exam tomorrow.
2 I don't think I'm confident. I'm usually quite _____.
3 My mother is always _____. She's not cheerful at all.
4 You're so _____ sometimes. Why can't you be more sensible?
5 When she was young, my cat was always active. Now she's just _____.

5 ⭐⭐ Circle the correct adjectives.

HOME | ABOUT ME | ARCHIVE | FOLLOW

My sister, Alicia, is a very ¹**confident** / talented person because she's always sure about herself and knows what she's good at. In fact, she's quite ²active / ambitious – she's got lots of goals and things she wants to achieve. She's also smart and really ³patient / talented – she can play the piano and is very good at sport. The only 'problem' is that she's not very ⁴cheerful / sociable – she doesn't like going to parties and she doesn't have many friends. But if I have a problem, she's always ⁵helpful / calm and tries to solve it. Alicia is ⁶sensitive / patient, too – she doesn't get angry, even when other people make really big mistakes. My sister is my hero!

Explore it!

Guess the correct answer.
Scientists believe that people who are _____ live longer than average.

a cheerful   b confident   c grumpy

Find an interesting fact about how to live longer and send the question in an email to a classmate or ask them in the next class.

READING
An article

1 ⭐ **Read the article quickly and answer the questions.**
   1 What is the name of the young man in photo A?
   _____
   2 What is the name of the wave in photo B?
   _____

2 ⭐⭐ **Match the words in bold in the article with the definitions.**
   1 very surprised _amazed_
   2 a physical or mental power to do something
   _____
   3 a person who teaches other people _____
   4 water that moves over the top of the sea _____
   5 very difficult _____
   6 wanting to do something very much _____

3 ⭐⭐ **Are the sentences T (true) or F (false)? Correct the false sentences.**
   1 Derek's favourite surfer was also called Derek.
   F. Derek's father's favourite surfer was also called
   Derek.
   2 Derek didn't surf until he was a teenager.
   _____
   3 Derek's father taught Derek to surf.
   _____
   4 Derek can hear which direction he needs to surf in.
   _____
   5 People who saw Derek in Hawaii were very surprised.
   _____
   6 Derek went to Hawaii to make a film with a producer.
   _____

4 ⭐⭐⭐ **Answer the questions in your own words.**
   1 Why do you think Derek was determined to try surfing?
   _____
   2 What do you think inspired the film producer to make a film about Derek?
   _____

Home   Posts   Archives

SURF WITHOUT SIGHT

Derek Rabelo was born in Brazil in 1992. His father called him Derek after a famous surfing champion, Derek Ho – his father's favourite surfer. Derek's father wanted Derek to become a surfer, too, but there was a problem: unfortunately, Derek was born blind. His father's dream to see his son surf seemed impossible!

When Derek was 17, his father told him about his dream. From that moment, Derek was **determined** to try to become a surfer. He went to the beach with his father every day and started taking surfing lessons with an **instructor**. Derek kept trying and finally, he learned to surf!

Derek explains that although he can't see, he understands the noises that the **waves** make and he can hear them when they are coming. He says every part of a wave makes a different noise, so he knows which direction to surf in.

In 2012, he flew to Hawaii to surf the famous Banzai Pipeline – one of the most **challenging** and dangerous waves in the world. Local surfers were **amazed** to see the confident young blind man surf the huge wave with no problem at all.

While Derek was surfing in Hawaii, he met a film producer who believed that Derek had an amazing **ability**. The producer decided to make a film about him. *Beyond Sight* tells Derek's inspirational story and teaches us that nothing is impossible if you believe in yourself!

LANGUAGE IN ACTION
Past simple and past continuous with *when*, *while* and *as*

1 ★ Complete the sentences with the past continuous form of the verbs in the box.

> do   look   not watch
> rain   ~~sleep~~   work

1 I __was sleeping__ at 11 o'clock last night. That's why I didn't check my emails.
2 It _____ yesterday, so I didn't go out.
3 My mum _____ late at the office and came home late.
4 I _____ for clothes online, but I didn't see anything I liked.
5 What _____ you _____ in the kitchen? I heard a strange noise.
6 She _____ videos on the computer – she was studying!

2 ★★ Complete the conversation with the past simple form of the verbs in brackets.

EMMA Hey, Ben! ¹ _Did you have_ (you / have) a nice holiday?
BEN Hmm, not bad. I ² _____ (help) my uncle in his shop.
EMMA Why ³ _____ (you / do) that?
BEN Because my aunt ⁴ _____ (be) ill, and he ⁵ _____ (not have) time to go to the shop every day.
EMMA Wow! That's really kind of you. ⁶ _____ (it / be) difficult?
BEN Yeah. But my uncle ⁷ _____ (give) me some money after, so I ⁸ _____ (buy) some new clothes.
EMMA Cool!

3 ★★ Write sentences with the past simple and past continuous and the words in brackets.

1 I / sleep / you / call / me last night (when)
   I was sleeping when you called me last night.
2 he / finish / his book / he / wait / for the bus (as)
   _____
3 we / live / in London / we / go / to lots of museums (while)
   _____
4 she / not see / the car / she / cross / the street (when)
   _____
5 I / not cry / I / watch / that inspirational film (while)
   _____
6 they / say / goodbye / they / leave / the party (as)
   _____

4 ★★ Circle the correct options.

One day my wife was ill, so I ¹(drove) / was driving to the chemist to get some medicine. While I ²walked / was walking back to the car, I noticed that I ³didn't have / wasn't having my keys. They were still in the car with my phone! I ⁴kicked / was kicking the wheels of my car when a teenager ⁵was arriving / arrived on his bike and ⁶asked / was asking what was wrong. I told him the story and I ⁷explained / was explaining that we had another car key at home, but it was five miles away. The boy said, 'I'll get the keys' and then ⁸gave / was giving me his phone to call my wife to explain what was happening. After 30 minutes, he ⁹came / was coming back with the keys. As I ¹⁰opened / was opening my car, he rode away – before I could thank him!

5 ★★★ Write a short paragraph in your notebook about a time when someone helped you or you helped someone. Use the past simple and past continuous.

VOCABULARY AND LISTENING
Phrasal verbs

1 ★ Circle the correct options.
1 If you have a good relationship with someone, you *get on* / *hang out* with them.
2 When you look after someone who is old, ill or very young, you *cheer up* / *take care* of them.
3 When you spend time with friends, you *hang out* / *deal* with them.
4 When you try to solve a problem, you *deal with* / *depend on* it.
5 If you respect and admire someone, you *look up to* / *give up* them.
6 When you make someone feel happier, you *cheer them up* / *hang them out*.
7 When you stop trying to do something because it is too difficult, you *cheer up* / *give up*.
8 When you need someone's help and support, you *look up to* / *depend on* them.

2 ★★ Complete the sentences with the phrasal verbs from Exercise 1.
1 I can't go out tonight. I have a lot of problems that I need to __deal with__ .
2 I sometimes _____ my little brother when my parents are not at home.
3 I can't do this homework – it's too difficult. I _____ !
4 I really _____ my mother. I think she's an amazing woman, and I'd like to be the same as her when I'm older.
5 I _____ my sister for help and advice. I often don't know what to do without her.
6 My grandfather is feeling sad these days, so I'm trying to _____ him _____ .
7 I usually _____ with friends at the park, or in a café.
8 Paula doesn't _____ with Susana very well. They're very different people.

A conversation

3 ★ Listen to the conversation. Why is Callum going to a concert?
a It's a family member's birthday.
b He wants to help people.
c It's his weekend job.

4 ★★ Listen again. Complete the notes with key words and information.

Concert
• Takes place at ¹ __the sports centre__
• Brandon's ² _____ ill in the past, concert to make money for people with same illness.
• Brandon wants to make a minimum of ³£_____ for charity.

Charity work
• Brandon made more than ⁴£_____ last month for charity.
• Jobs he did: washed ⁵_____, cut grass in gardens, took rubbish away.
• Worked every afternoon and ⁶_____ .

5 ★★★ Callum mentions running a race, giving up chocolate and cutting off his hair for charity. Think of three other ways to raise money.
1 _____
2 _____
3 _____

LANGUAGE IN ACTION
used to

1 ⭐ **Match sentences 1–6 with a–f.**
1. I used to live in the countryside. `c`
2. I didn't use to like coffee. ☐
3. I used to be really shy. ☐
4. I used to like going to the gym. ☐
5. I used to eat a lot of fast food. ☐
6. I didn't use to have many friends. ☐

a Now I don't have time.
b Now I think it's unhealthy.
c I live in a city now.
d Now I have lots.
e I'm much more confident these days.
f Now I have a cup every morning.

2 ⭐ **Complete the text with *used to* or *didn't use to*.**

When I was very young, I ¹ _used to_ want to be a swimming teacher, because I loved swimming and I ² _____ like our sports teacher. Sometimes, I ³ _____ want to be an astronaut as well, because I really liked space. When I got older, I started to get interested in computers. We ⁴ _____ have a good computer at home, only a very old one, but then my dad decided to buy a really good one. My parents ⁵ _____ let me spend much time on the computer – just a few hours a week. When I was 13, I started learning how to write my own games. I ⁶ _____ know how to do that before, but I had a great teacher at school who showed me how. In the future, I'd like to be a games developer!

3 ⭐⭐ **Look at the photos. Complete the sentences with the correct form of *used to*.**
1. I _didn't use to like ice cream_, but now I love it!
2. I _____, but I play tennis now.
3. I _____, but now I want to be a teacher.
4. I _____, but I have one now.
5. I _____. Now I have a new one.

4 ⭐⭐ **Put the words in the correct order to make questions with *used to*.**
1. you / use / to / Did / mobile phones / have / ?
   Did you use to have mobile phones?
2. did / How / communicate / with / people / use / to / you / ?
   _____
3. free / in / your / What / you / did / use / do / to / time / ?
   _____
4. old / use / people / What / you / think / did / of / to / ?
   _____

5 ⭐⭐ **Complete the answers to the questions from Exercise 4. Use the correct form of *used to* and the verbs in the box.**

> be   do   have (x2)   read   send   think (x2)

1. Well, no. I got my first mobile phone 15 years ago. Before that, we _didn't use to have_ the internet or even computers. We _____ a phone at home, of course.
2. We _____ letters, phone each other or just meet up a lot. Life _____ calmer then.
3. I watched TV. I _____ a lot of books, too. A lot of people now go shopping. We _____ that because we didn't have the money.
4. Good question! I _____ about them at all! I _____ I couldn't get old. I still don't think I'm old!

12 BE INSPIRED | UNIT 1

WRITING
A letter to a magazine

1 ⭐ Read the competition details. What is the prize for the best entry? _____

Competition! Write and tell us about a helpful person in your life who you think deserves an award. As always, the winning letter appears online in next month's edition and receives £100! Answer the following questions.
- Who is the most helpful person you know?
- What do/did they do to help you?
- Why do you think they deserve to win an award?

2 ⭐ Read the letter to a magazine. Does the writer answer the questions in Exercise 1 in the same order? _____

3 ⭐⭐ Complete the *Useful language* phrases in the letter to a magazine with the words in the box.

> For   view   ~~opinion~~   Personally

4 ⭐⭐ Read the letter again. Are the sentences *T* (true) or *F* (false)?

1 The writer wasn't very happy at her old school. __F__
2 She went to a new school because her parents wanted to live in the countryside. ____
3 Her teacher asked her easy questions in class to help her. ____
4 The writer thinks Mrs Davies should win the award because she helped build her confidence. ____

The most helpful person I know is my English teacher, Mrs Davies. In my ¹ _opinion_ , she should definitely win an award. Here's why.

A few years ago, I used to go to a different school and I liked it very much. Then my parents got new jobs in a different city and I changed schools. In the new school, I was shy and not at all confident. I didn't make any new friends. The only person who really noticed this was Mrs Davies. She helped me by talking to me in the class, and putting me in groups with other friendly students. She also often asked questions that she knew I could answer in front of the class. ² _____ me, that was a very kind thing to do. ³ _____ , I think I became more confident and sociable because of Mrs Davies!

In my ⁴ _____ , Mrs Davies deserves an award because she's the calmest and most patient teacher at our school. She's also sensitive to people's feelings and always wants to help her students. She helped me in a difficult situation and she also inspired me to like English!

Write your own letter to a magazine.

PLAN

5 ⭐⭐ Think of a helpful person you know. What do/did they do to help you? Why should they win the competition?

WRITE

6 ⭐⭐⭐ Write your letter. Remember to include three paragraphs, past tenses, *used to* and phrases from the *Useful language* box (see Student's Book, p17).

CHECK

7 Do you …
- introduce the person in the first paragraph?
- say why the person should win?
- use language for giving opinions?

UNIT 1 | BE INSPIRED 13

1 REVIEW

VOCABULARY

1 Match the people with the adjectives in the box.

> active   ambitious   calm   cheerful
> confident   helpful   inspiring   patient
> sensible   sensitive   sociable   talented

1 She runs every morning and goes to the gym at the weekend, too! _____
2 Mark always wants to do things for other people. _____
3 He never gets nervous. He always looks relaxed. _____
4 Sara can play the piano very well. She's also an amazing singer. _____
5 Paula loves talking to people and making new friends. _____
6 John is 100% sure about everything he does – he believes he can do anything. _____
7 I was 45 minutes late, but Ashraf didn't get angry at all! _____
8 We all look up to George. He's an amazing person. _____
9 Kerry is always playing tennis. She wants to be a professional player one day. _____
10 Linda is always smiling, even when everyone else is sad or tired. _____
11 Be careful what you say to Hannah. She gets upset very easily. _____
12 Johann is a serious person. He always says and does the right thing. _____

2 Circle the correct prepositions.

1 I always looked up *with / to* my older brother when I was young.
2 Don't look so sad. Cheer *to / up*!
3 I might go out today. It depends *on / of* the weather.
4 I tried running five kilometres yesterday, but I was tired and gave *up / out* after four kilometres.
5 You need to be very patient to deal *with / on* little children.
6 Everyone gets *in / on* with John because he's really cheerful and sociable.
7 I was hanging *out / on* with my friends last night.
8 I used to take care *with / of* my little sister when she was a baby.

LANGUAGE IN ACTION

3 Complete the sentences with the past simple and past continuous form of the verbs in brackets.

1 I _____ (walk) to the shops when it _____ (start) to rain.
2 My friend _____ (phone) me as I _____ (write) him a text.
3 What _____ Harry and Abby _____ (do) when they _____ (hear) the news?
4 He _____ (find) an expensive ring when he _____ (clean) their house.
5 We _____ (leave) Tom's house when Lisa _____ (arrive).
6 As I _____ (cross) the road, a woman _____ (hit) me with her bike!

14 BE INSPIRED | UNIT 1

4 Complete the conversation with the correct form of *used to* and the verbs in brackets.

A How old is your brother now?
B He's nine.
A Wow! I remember him when he ¹_____ (be) a little baby.
B Yes. And I ²_____ (take) care of him, too! I ³_____ (read) him bedtime stories!
A ⁴_____ (you / give) him food and put him to bed?
B No, I ⁵_____ (not do) that. My parents ⁶_____ (do) it. He's changed a lot. He really ⁷_____ (look) up to me, but now he doesn't!

CUMULATIVE LANGUAGE

5 Complete the text with the missing words. (Circle) the correct options.

When my mother was younger, she ¹_____ a singer. I ²_____ this until recently! She ³_____ long, blonde hair, and she ⁴_____ really strange clothes. In her first year at university, she ⁵_____ some other people who wanted to form a band. The other people quickly ⁶_____ out that she was a really talented singer, so they asked her to join in. She ⁷_____ famous, or anything like that, but she had a lot of fun. Unfortunately, I ⁸_____ any recordings of her singing. They ⁹_____ phones or video cameras then, so I can't see what she looked like. It's difficult to believe that my mum used to be a singer, because she ¹⁰_____ very serious and sensible these days! She's got short, dark hair and she ¹¹_____ in a bank! Where did that young pop singer ¹²_____ ?

1 a	is	b	was being	c	was
2 a	not know	b	didn't knew	c	didn't know
3 a	was having	b	did have	c	used to have
4 a	wore	b	was wearing	c	wear
5 a	was meeting	b	met	c	meets
6 a	found	b	find	c	were finding
7 a	weren't	b	wasn't being	c	didn't use to be
8 a	haven't got	b	have not	c	hasn't got
9 a	weren't having	b	didn't used to have	c	didn't use to have
10 a	always	b	is always	c	always is
11 a	works	b	usually works	c	work
12 a	goes	b	went	c	go

2 WHAT IS ART?

VOCABULARY
Visual and performing arts

1 ★ Complete the visual and performing arts words. Then match the words with photos a–h.

1 filmmaking — d
2 s _ _ ee _ a _ t
3 _ o _ e _ _ o a y _ a _ _ e
4 _ a _ _ io _ _ e _ i _ n
5 s _ u _ p _ u _ e
6 p _ _ o _ o _ _ a _ h _
7 a _ c _ i _ e _ _ u _ e
8 i _ _ u _ t _ a _ io _

2 ★★ Correct the sentences by changing the underlined words.

1 You see paintings and other art forms in <u>a performance</u>. _____
2 <u>A gallery</u> is an inside or outside event where you can see paintings and other art forms. _____
3 <u>An exhibition</u> is the action of entertaining people by dancing, singing, acting or playing music. _____

3 ★★ Match the beginnings of the words with the ends to make the names of the people who do an activity.

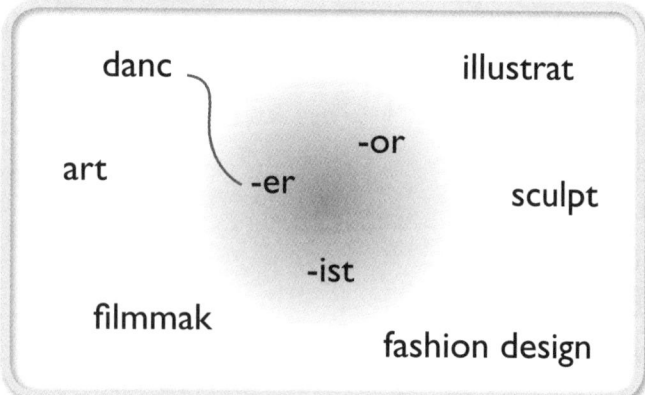

danc / illustrat / art / sculpt / filmmak / fashion design
-or / -er / -ist

4 ★★ Match the people or things (1–6) with the definitions (a–f).

1 contemporary dance — e
2 fashion design
3 street art
4 filmmaker
5 sculpture
6 illustrator

a making objects that represent things, people or ideas
b someone who draws pictures for books
c someone who creates movies for TV or cinema
d working with clothes, shoes and sometimes hairstyles
e moving to music in a modern style
f paintings, graffiti, etc. outside in urban areas

Explore it!

Guess the correct answer.

Every _____ minutes, people around the world take more photos than the whole of humanity took in the 1800s.

a 2 b 10 c 45

Find an interesting fact about an art form and send the question in an email to a classmate or ask them in the next class.

READING
A magazine article

1 ★ Look at the photo. What art form can you see and where do you think it is?

_____

2 ★ Read the article from an art magazine and check your answer to Exercise 1.

3 ★★ Match the words in bold in the article with the definitions.
1 going under water   _sinking_
2 people who work to protect the environment _____
3 a dark orange-brown metal _____
4 put something into position _____
5 an ability to achieve something _____
6 keep or maintain something in its position _____

4 ★★ Read the article again. Answer the questions.
1 Where did Lorenzo Quinn study art?
   In the USA.
2 What are Quinn's sculptures normally made from?
   _____
3 Which important problem does *Support* deal with?
   _____
4 How are the giant hands 'helping' the Ca' Sagredo Hotel?
   _____
5 How did Quinn's family help with *Support*?
   _____
6 Who can do something about climate change, according to Quinn?
   _____

5 ★★★ Answer the questions in your own words.
1 What's your favourite form of art? Why do you like it?
   _____
   _____
2 What other important issues does art often deal with? Think of two examples.
   _____
   _____

Support: an art installation

Sculptor Lorenzo Quinn is the first artist to **install** a work of art directly into the Grand Canal in Venice. But who is he and what does his work of art mean?

Quinn was born in Rome, but he has lived in Spain and in the USA, where he studied art. He hasn't always been a sculptor. He has also been a singer and he has acted in films – once as the painter Salvador Dalí!

His sculptures have appeared at exhibitions internationally. He usually works with metals such as **bronze**, steel and aluminium. But what inspired him to make visual art with two enormous hands?

Together with many scientists and **conservationists**, Quinn believes that the Mediterranean Sea has risen and is still rising because of climate change. Because of higher water levels in the Grand Canal, the historic city of Venice is slowly **sinking**, they believe.

The art installation, called *Support*, which Quinn created for the Venice Art Biennale exhibition, warns us about the danger of rising water levels in this amazing city. The two giant hands **'hold up'** the famous Ca' Sagredo Hotel on Venice's Grand Canal.

Quinn used his son's hands as models for the huge sculptures, to show the **potential** of the next generation. The message is that the future is in their hands.

UNIT 2 | WHAT IS ART? 17

LANGUAGE IN ACTION
Present perfect with regular and irregular verbs

1 ★ Circle the correct options.
1. He has *use* / *used* bronze to make the sculpture.
2. *Have* / *Has* you watched that video about Dalí?
3. They haven't *visit* / *visited* many exhibitions.
4. I have never *meet* / *met* a street artist.
5. *Has* / *Have* your art teacher taught you how to use spray paint?
6. A: Have they visited the new gallery?
   B: Yes, they *have* / *haven't*.

2 ★ Complete the sentences with the present perfect form of the verbs in brackets.
1. We _have been_ (be) to a very interesting exhibition.
2. She _____ (not do) any contemporary dance.
3. The children _____ (make) some plastic models.
4. I _____ (see) some lovely artwork today.
5. _____ you _____ (take) the artist's name and number?
6. Safi's mum _____ (write) to her art teacher.

3 ★★ Complete the sentences with the present perfect form of the verbs in the box.

| be   draw   ~~have~~   make   not see   not write |

1. The art installation _has had_ an enormous number of visitors.
2. We _____ the new exhibition yet.
3. _____ Lorenzo Quinn _____ any new sculptures this year?
4. My favourite singer _____ many good songs this year.
5. _____ you ever _____ a picture of a rabbit? It isn't easy!
6. I _____ never _____ on a gondola on the Grand Canal. Have you?

4 ★★ Complete the sentences with *been* or *gone*.
1. I've _been_ to the art shop. Look what I bought.
2. Helena's _____ into town but she's normally back home by 5 o'clock.
3. My parents have _____ to Venice lots of times.
4. We've _____ to see the exhibition and we loved it.
5. He's _____ to the gallery. He's meeting the artist.

5 ★★ Write questions and answers.
1. your brother / ever read / *Death in Venice* / ?
   No / see / the film
   Has your brother ever read Death in Venice?
   No, he hasn't, but he has seen the film.
2. they / ever visit / Rio / ?
   No / be / to São Paulo
   _____
   _____
3. she / ever win / first prize in a competition / ?
   No / come / second
   _____
   _____
4. you / ever make / a video film / ?
   No / take / some great photos on my phone
   _____
   _____

6 ★★★ Complete the text with the present perfect form of the verbs in the box.

| change   ever have   ~~join~~   make   train |

JOIN OUR SALSA FREEDOM DANCE CLASSES!
Read what some of our students wrote about it:

'My friends and I [1] _have joined_ many different classes, but the salsa class is the best – it's brilliant!'

'This is the best class I [2] _____. Everyone is so welcoming. I [3] _____ some great new friends.'

'Salsa dancing [4] _____ my life! My teacher [5] _____ in Colombia and the Caribbean and her classes are fun and very exciting!'

VOCABULARY AND LISTENING
Music and theatre

1 ☆ **Match the beginnings of the sentences (1–6) with the ends (a–f).**

1 The words of a song — c
2 A recording studio is where
3 The words an actor says
4 The audience are the people
5 You have an audition when
6 During a rehearsal

a who listen to the orchestra.
b you want a part or role in a play or show.
c are called the lyrics.
d you practise a play, concert or show.
e are called the lines.
f singers and musicians record their music.

2 ☆ **Circle the correct options.**

1 When the *orchestra* / *audience* stopped playing their instruments, we stood up and clapped.
2 In the final *show* / *scene*, the friends say goodbye and the film finishes.
3 I really want the *line* / *part* of Romeo in the school production of *Romeo and Juliet*.
4 What's your favourite type of *part* / *show*: dance, music or theatre?

3 ☆☆☆ **Answer the questions.**

1 Have you ever written lyrics for a song? What was the song about?

2 Have you ever performed in a play or a show? What part did you have?

3 Have you ever played in or been to see an orchestra? Which one?

A conversation

4 🎧 2.01 ☆☆ **Listen to Melanie and David talking about Alma Deutscher, a young musician. Answer the questions.**

1 How does Melanie feel about Alma at the beginning of the conversation? _____
2 Does she feel differently at the end? _____

5 🎧 2.01 ☆☆ **Listen again and answer the questions.**

1 How does David know so much about Alma Deutscher?
   He watched a programme about her on YouTube.
2 What art form is Alma's *Cinderella*?

3 What musical instruments does Alma play?

4 Where was the performance of *Cinderella*?

5 How does Alma get some of her ideas and melodies?

6 What activity is a waste of time, according to Alma?

6 ☆☆☆ **Find out about another talented young person like Alma Deutscher. Write a short paragraph about their life and achievements in your notebook.**

LANGUAGE IN ACTION
Present perfect with *already, just, still* and *yet*

1 ★ Match sentences 1–6 with a–f.
1 My mum's just found her glasses. [c]
2 I haven't seen that film yet. [ ]
3 The show has already started. [ ]
4 She still hasn't heard from Joel. [ ]
5 I've just had a second audition. [ ]
6 The children haven't gone to bed yet. [ ]

a She hopes he calls soon.
b I hope I get the part.
c Now she can see the stage.
d They'll be tired in the morning.
e We've missed the beginning.
f We've got tickets to see it tomorrow.

2 ★★ Look at the photos. Write sentences about what has just happened.

1 she / cut his hair
She has just cut his hair.
2 The children / finish school for the day
3 they / have a swim
4 he / make a cake
5 the girls / see a funny film
6 the boy / give her some flowers

3 ★★ Circle the letter for the correct sentence.
1 A I've already seen the art exhibition.
  B Already I've seen the art exhibition.
2 A Dylan just has left for school.
  B Dylan has just left for school.
3 A She hasn't tidied her room still!
  B She still hasn't tidied her room!
4 A Have you bought the orchestra tickets yet?
  B Have you bought yet the orchestra tickets?
5 A Lay and Eva have come back from the cinema just.
  B Lay and Eva have just come back from the cinema.

4 ★★ Rewrite the sentences putting the words in brackets in the correct position.
1 Hey, the gallery has announced an exciting event. (just)
Hey, the gallery has just announced an exciting event.
2 Have you heard about the Picasso exhibition? (yet)
3 Someone has discovered an unknown painting. (just)
4 The gallery has bought it from a collector in Paris. (just)
5 It seems they have agreed a fair price. (already)
6 They haven't told anyone how much they paid, though. (still)

5 ★★★ Put the words in the correct order to make sentences and questions.
1 you / yet / seen / new / the / Shrek film / Have / ?
Have you seen the new Shrek film yet?
2 art gallery / already / to / Enzo / the / has / gone / .
3 still / art project / finished / Susie / her / hasn't / .
4 audition / you / your / had / yet / Have / ?
5 have / They / in town / just / held / an exhibition / .
6 three times / been / have / We / to / already / the theatre / this month / !

WRITING
A review

1 ⭐ Look at the photo. (Circle) the correct answer.
The New Dance School is …
a a classical orchestra.   c a group of dancers.
b a music group.

2 ⭐ Read the review. Why does the reviewer recommend The New Dance School?

A Have you seen The New Dance School yet? I've never heard anything like it before. The band is perfect for lovers of international music — it's the best performance I've ever been to!

B The New Dance School's music isn't exactly rock. It's a bit like world music, but you can really dance to it! The musicians are all really talented. They create powerful rhythms with a number of different instruments, like sitars, bongos and steel drums — it's amazing.

C What I liked about it was that the performers were so happy and there was a lot of movement in their music. They make you feel cheerful. I was sitting in the audience, but I really wanted to get up and dance!

D I saw them at my local village hall. It was so cool! These musicians haven't been together very long, but they have a big future! The next New Dance School concert is on at the Edale Music Festival, so don't miss it. I recommend it because the music has great energy and it makes you want to dance.

3 ⭐ Which paragraph (A–D) …
1 gives a description of the band and its music? _B_
2 explains what the reviewer liked / didn't like about it? ___
3 gives details of where you can see the band? ___
4 explains who the band's audience is? ___

4 ⭐ (Circle) the correct words in the *Useful language* phrases. Then check in the review.
1 I've (never) / ever heard anything like it before.
2 It's *in* / *on* at …
3 I *recommend* / *recommending* it because …
4 It's the best performance I've *ever* / *never* been to.
5 *How* / *What* I liked / didn't like about it was …

5 ⭐⭐ Read the review again. Answer the questions.
1 Who is the concert for, in the reviewer's opinion?
_____
2 What does the reviewer like best about the band?
_____

Write your own review of a music concert.

PLAN

6 ⭐⭐ Make notes on a music concert you have been to or seen on TV.

Where did you see it? _____
Who was the concert for? _____
What was it like? _____
What did you like / not like about it? _____

7 Decide what information to include in each paragraph. Use the information in Exercise 3 to help you.

WRITE

8 ⭐⭐⭐ Write your review. Remember to include four paragraphs, the present perfect and phrases from the *Useful language* box (see Student's Book, p29).

CHECK

9 Do you …
• describe the event?
• say who it is for?
• say what you liked / didn't like about it?

UNIT 2 | WHAT IS ART? 21

2 REVIEW

VOCABULARY

1 Complete the sentences with the words in the box.

> architecture   contemporary dance   exhibition
> filmmaking   illustrations   performance
> photography   sculptures   street art   gallery

1 Eduardo goes to the cinema a lot because he's interested in _____.
2 Lorenzo Quinn makes _____ of people and things from different metals.
3 I love _____, but you need a lot of energy and rhythm to move your body to the music.
4 The Louvre in Paris is the most famous art _____ in the world – the *Mona Lisa* is there.
5 They saw a wonderful _____ of paintings and sculptures by a local artist.
6 The _____ in this book are in black and white, not colour.
7 We saw a _____ of *High School Musical* at our local theatre – it was quite good.
8 I bought a new camera for my _____ class. I've taken some great pictures.
9 _____ is to design, plan and make buildings.
10 Some _____ is OK, but I really don't like graffiti. It looks messy.

2 Read the definitions and complete the words.

1 (n) o_____: a big group of musicians who play different instruments together

2 (n) p_____: one of the people in a film, play or dance

3 (n) s_____: a part of a play or film in which the action happens in one place

4 (n) a_____: the group of people together in one place to watch or listen to a play, film, etc.

LANGUAGE IN ACTION

3 Write questions and short answers (affirmative or negative) in the present perfect.

1 you / see the new Almodóvar movie? (✓)
   _____
2 he / take photos of his sculpture? (✓)
   _____
3 the visitors / come from all over the world? (✗)
   _____
4 she / ever sing in front of a big audience? (✗)
   _____
5 they / hear your new song? (✓)
   _____
6 you / have many exhibitions? (✗)
   _____
7 she / be to that gallery before? (✓)
   _____
8 the show / win many awards? (✗)
   _____

5 (n) a_____: a short performance that an actor, dancer, etc. gives to show they can play a particular part

6 (n) l_____: the words of a song

7 (n) r_____: the time when all the people in a play, dance, etc. practise to prepare for a performance

8 (n) l_____: the words that an actor speaks when performing in a film, play, etc.

9 (n) s_____: a theatre performance or a television or radio programme

10 (n) r_____ s_____: a place where a musician makes and records their songs

22 WHAT IS ART? | UNIT 2

4 Make the sentences negative using the words in brackets.

1 I've just done my homework. (not yet)
_____

2 He's read that book already. (still not)
_____

3 We've been to Venice. (still not)
_____

4 The performance has just begun. (not yet)
_____

5 The sculptor has explained his work. (still not)
_____

6 We've just bought your new CD. (not yet)
_____

7 She's just met the photographer. (still not)
_____

8 I've been into Paul's recording studio. (not yet)
_____

CUMULATIVE LANGUAGE

5 Complete the conversation with the missing words. (Circle) the correct options.

INTERVIEWER	Hello and welcome. We've got some great music for you today, but I ¹_____ that one of our most talented young singers, Lexi West, is in the recording studio. Welcome to London, Lexi!
LEXI	Thanks! It's great to be here. Actually, I ²_____ a house in the city. It's all very new and exciting for me!
INTERVIEWER	Yeah? Where ³_____ live? You were born in Scotland, right? But of course you ⁴_____ all over the world.
LEXI	That's right. I ⁵_____ back from New York, but while I ⁶_____ and working abroad, I didn't have my own place. I ⁷_____ with my parents.
INTERVIEWER	Was there a lot of music in your home when you ⁸_____, Lexi? I believe your father ⁹_____ songs for you.
LEXI	Yes, that's right. My dad was definitely my inspiration, but he was also very sensible. I ¹⁰_____ on TV as a teenager, but he never let me miss school! I still ¹¹_____ his advice: it's OK to be ambitious but don't get impatient!
INTERVIEWER	Well, Lexi, you ¹²_____ three number one hits, so you didn't have to wait very long to be famous!

1 a 've still heard   b haven't heard   c 've just heard
2 a didn't buy   b 've just bought   c was just buying
3 a did you use to   b were you used to   c use you to
4 a haven't travelled   b 've travelled   c weren't travelling
5 a was coming   b have already come   c 've just come
6 a was singing   b wasn't singing   c used to sing
7 a didn't use to   b was living   c haven't lived
8 a have grown up   b grew up   c were growing up
9 a has just written   b didn't use to write   c used to write
10 a performing   b was performing   c have just performed
11 a used to forget   b was forgetting   c haven't forgotten
12 a 've already had   b haven't had   c were having

3 SPREAD THE WORD!

VOCABULARY
Communicating

1 ⭐ Put the letters in order to make words about communicating.

1 tereg — g r e e t
2 retgesu — g_____
3 besiredc — d_____
4 ptreertin — i_____
5 stpo — p____
6 eksha nsdah — s_____ h____
7 leims — s____
8 vewa — w____
9 latsenrta — t_____
10 wrheips — w_____
11 tsuho — s____

2 ⭐⭐ Complete the sentences with words from Exercise 1.

1 A thumbs up sign is a _gesture_ that means 'good'.
2 I don't know what Jackie looks like. Can you _____ her to me?
3 Don't speak loudly. Please _____. You'll wake up the baby.
4 These instructions are in French. I need someone to _____ them for me.
5 There's Lucy across the road. Let's _____ at her. Maybe she will see us.
6 I only _____ when I'm very angry.
7 Everyone understands when you _____ at them. It means you're happy.
8 It's good to _____ comments online and then wait for people to reply to them.

3 ⭐⭐ Complete the spidergrams with words from Exercise 1.

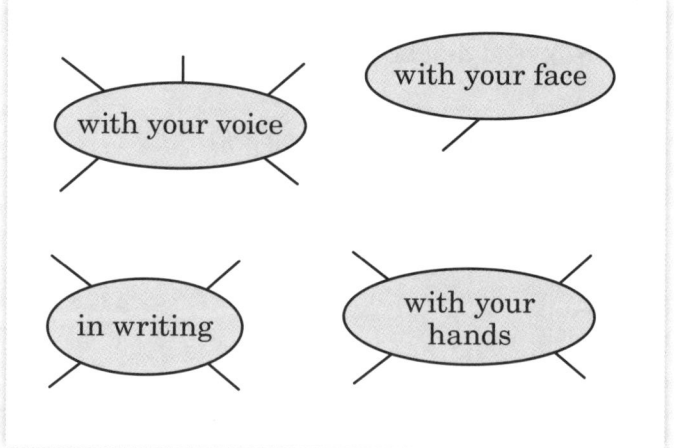

4 ⭐⭐ Complete the story with the correct form of words from Exercise 1.

I met my friend Kazue yesterday for the first time! Actually, I first met her online about six months ago. She's from Japan and now she's visiting my country with her family. I ¹ _greeted_ her at the airport when she arrived. In her emails, she ² _____ herself as quite small, but in fact she's as tall as me. I also met her brother and her parents. I wanted to ³ _____ hands with them, but Kazue quietly ⁴ _____ in my ear that Japanese people don't usually do that when they meet. I already knew what her brother looked like, because Kazue sometimes ⁵ _____ photos of him online. He was very friendly and he ⁶ _____ a lot. Kazue's parents don't speak English, but Kazue ⁷ _____ everything I said into Japanese. Kazue and her family were tired and wanted to go to their hotel. I arranged to meet Kazue the next day and we ⁸ _____ goodbye as they drove away in a taxi.

Explore it!

Guess the correct answer.

People originally shook hands because …

a they wanted to find out how strong the other person was.
b they wanted to show that they didn't want to start a fight.
c they wanted to check that the other person had clean hands.

Find an interesting fact about greetings and send the question in an email to a classmate or ask them in the next class.

24 SPREAD THE WORD! | UNIT 3

READING
An article

1 ⭐ Look at the photo. What emotions/actions do the emojis show? _____

2 ⭐ Read the article and complete the paragraphs (A–D) with the headings (1–4).
   1 From Japan to the world
   2 The most popular symbol
   3 Japan's alphabets
   4 A world language

3 ⭐ Find adverbs in the article with the meanings below.
   1 in a good way (paragraph A) ____well____
   2 with no problems (paragraph B) _____
   3 very much (paragraph C) _____
   4 not how you expect (paragraph D) _____

4 ⭐⭐ Read the article again. Are the sentences T (true) or F (false)? Correct the false sentences.
   1 For verb endings like -ing, Japanese people use the hiragana alphabet.
      ____T____
   2 Katakana has got the most symbols.
      _____
   3 You can't use more than one alphabet in one text.
      _____
   4 The first emoji didn't express many different feelings.
      _____
   5 In paragraph C, 'ones' refers to 'people'.
      _____
   6 The writer hopes emoji will become an international language in the future.
      _____

5 ⭐⭐⭐ Answer the questions in your own words.
   1 Which emoji do you use most often? Why?
      _____
   2 Apart from using emoji, how else can we show emotions in text messages?
      _____
   3 Is the alphabet in your language different from English? How?
      _____

Emoji
the world's most popular alphabet?

A _____

Did you know that the Japanese language has three alphabets? One alphabet, *katakana*, is mostly for foreign words, like 'pizza' (ピザ). This alphabet has 48 characters, or letters and symbols. Another alphabet, *hiragana*, is usually for grammar words, like the word ending 'した', which changes a verb into the past tense – similar to -ed in English. *Hiragana* has 46 characters. A third alphabet, *kanji*, has about 50,000 different symbols. It is usually for verbs, adjectives and nouns. For example, '山' is the Japanese symbol for 'mountain'. Often a piece of writing contains all three alphabets at the same time! Learning written Japanese well can be difficult!

B _____

But there is another kind of 'alphabet' from Japan, which everyone can easily recognise. You probably use it a lot when you communicate with friends. It doesn't use letters, it uses emoji, which translates as 'picture character' in English. We can all recognise emoji when we see them. They show a huge range of feelings or actions, from love and sadness to dancing and waving.

C _____

The Japanese have used emoji since 1999. Of course, these early emoji were very simple and people could only use them to show basic emotions. Since then, they have become more and more popular around the world and the number of emoji symbols has greatly increased – now there are nearly 3,000 official ones. Everyone can understand emoji – it doesn't matter which country they are from.

D _____

And what is the most common emoji symbol that people use? Surprisingly, it is not a smiling face or a heart. It is the 'tears of joy' emoji, showing a face laughing and crying happily. Perhaps in the future, they will create an emoji for every possible emotion and we will be able to communicate with anyone in the world, only by using emoji symbols!

LANGUAGE IN ACTION
can, could, will be able to

1 ★ **Are these sentences about the *past*, *present* or *future*?**

1. Most people couldn't send each other quick messages 30 years ago. _past_
2. It's possible that we will be able to interpret any language on a smartphone app. _____
3. Animals can't communicate in the same way that humans can. _____
4. I couldn't speak until I was three years old. _____
5. I won't be able to use my phone in the mountains. _____

2 ★★ **Complete the conversation with the correct form of *can*, *could* or *will be able to* and the verbs in brackets.**

KIM ¹ _Can you tell_ (you / tell) me why you didn't reply to my email?
DAN Sorry! I was at my grandparents' house in the middle of the countryside. I ² _____ (not use) my phone.
KIM Really? But you ³ _____ (post) messages online. I saw them.
DAN Err, yes, but I ⁴ _____ (not check) my emails.
KIM Right, anyway, ⁵ _____ (you / help) me practise my presentation tomorrow for next week's test?
DAN Sorry, I ⁶ _____ (not do) it then. I'm really busy. I ⁷ _____ (help) you now, though.
KIM Oh, I ⁸ _____ (not practise) now. I haven't written anything yet.
DAN Well, we ⁹ _____ (write) it together now, if you want. What's the topic of the presentation?
KIM How to communicate successfully!

3 ★★ **Complete the blogs with one word in each gap.**

HOME | ABOUT ME | ARCHIVE | FOLLOW

Julia
I ¹ _couldn't_ play the piano very well when I was younger. I didn't like practising because the piano was in our living room downstairs. That meant everyone had to listen to me when I played and no one ² _____ watch TV or read. Now I've got an electric piano and I ³ _____ use headphones. It's great because my family ⁴ _____ hear anything I'm playing! So now I'm practising a lot and I ⁵ _____ play quite well.

Liam
I ⁶ _____ swim at all, but I'd like to. Last summer, I went with my friends to the beach and I ⁷ _____ join in the fun in the water. That made me feel sad, so I hope I ⁸ _____ be able to start taking lessons in the next few months. I know that I ⁹ _____ be able to swim like a fish after just a few lessons, but I just want to be confident in the water so that I ¹⁰ _____ be able to swim with my friends next summer!

4 ★★★ **Look at the information about Olga. Write sentences with the correct form of *can*, *could* and *will be able to*.**

	1 play the piano	2 type quickly	3 sleep ten hours a night	4 ask her parents for money
when she was younger	✗		✓	
now	✓	✗	✗	✓
in the future		✓		✗

1. _Olga couldn't play the piano when she was younger, but she can now._
2. _____
3. _____
4. _____

26 SPREAD THE WORD! | UNIT 3

LISTENING AND VOCABULARY
A radio interview • Collocations with *say* and *tell*

1 ⭐⭐ **Listen to a radio interview about dolphins. Tick (✓) the topics that the people talk about.** 🎧 3.01
1. ☐ dolphin communication and language
2. ☐ dolphin greetings
3. ☐ the language of human babies
4. ☐ dolphin body language
5. ☐ how quickly dolphins can swim
6. ☐ new technology

2 ⭐⭐ **Listen again. Are the sentences T (true) or F (false)?** 🎧 3.01
1. Sara thinks that all dolphins speak the same language. __F__
2. Scientists believe dolphins have got names. _____
3. Dolphins talk to each other at the same time without stopping. _____
4. In one experiment, two dolphins spoke on a phone. _____
5. Dolphins can communicate over long distances. _____
6. Scientists have got the technology to translate what dolphins are saying. _____

3 ⭐ **Complete the flashcards with *say* or *tell*.**

1. _say_ hello
2. _____ sorry
3. _____ the truth
4. _____ a story
5. _____ a lie
6. _____ someone a secret
7. _____ yes/no
8. _____ (something) in Italian
9. _____ a joke

4 ⭐⭐ **Complete the sentences with the correct form of the collocations from Exercise 3.**
1. Can I _tell_ you a _secret_? But promise you won't tell anyone else.
2. How do you _____ 'thank you' _____?
3. Let me _____ you a _____ about how I met my best friend.
4. The interviewer asked me if I wanted the job. I _____, of course!
5. Maria says she hasn't got any money, but I don't think she's _____. She always wears expensive clothes.
6. I _____ to your brother in the street, but he didn't answer me and continued walking!
7. I like _____, but I can never make them sound funny.
8. I want to _____ for shouting at you last week.
9. Ed just _____ me a big _____. I'll never believe him again!

5 ⭐⭐⭐ **Answer the questions.**
1. Have you ever told a 'good' lie to help someone? What lie did you tell?

2. When you have a secret, who do you tell?

3. How many languages can you say something in? Which languages?

UNIT 3 | SPREAD THE WORD! 27

LANGUAGE IN ACTION

Present perfect with *for/since* and *How long ... ?*

1 ⭐ (Circle) the best ending for each sentence.
  1 I've lived here for …
    a two years.   b I was 14 years old.
  2 I've had this phone for …
    a a long time.   b 2015.
  3 I haven't eaten anything since …
    a about three hours.   b this morning.
  4 I've been able to speak French since …
    a 10 years ago.   b I was a child.
  5 My best friend and I have known each other for …
    a six years.   b we started school together.
  6 Max has been on the computer since …
    a all day.   b he woke up.

2 ⭐⭐ Complete the questions with *How long* and the present perfect form of the verbs in the box.

   | be   have   know   like   ~~live~~ |

  A ¹ _How long have you lived_ here?
  B For about six months. I really like it here. It's a nice city.
  A So Emma and Kirsty are friends? ² _____ each other?
  B Since they were about three years old. They've been best friends for ages!
  A I didn't know Olivia liked watching tennis. ³ _____ it?
  B For a long time. She's played in the school team since she was really young.
  A I see that Will's got a new bike. ⁴ _____ it?
  B For ages. He needed a new one. The old one was too small for him.
  A I'm sorry I'm late, everyone. ⁵ _____ here?
  B Not long. Don't worry. We only got here ten minutes ago.

Present perfect and past simple

3 ⭐⭐ Complete the joke with the past simple or present perfect form of the verbs in brackets.

My friend ¹ _told_ (tell) me a funny joke this morning. I ² _____ (hear) a lot of jokes in my life, but this one ³ _____ (make) me laugh when I ⁴ _____ (hear) it.
A girl and her father ⁵ _____ (be) at the dinner table, having some soup. The girl ⁶ _____ (ask) her dad, 'Dad, are spiders nice to eat?' 'What a horrible question,' ⁷ _____ (say) the father. 'Can't you think of anything nice to say at dinner time? Please let me eat. I ⁸ _____ (eat not) anything since this morning!' The girl ⁹ _____ (decide) to be quiet. They both ¹⁰ _____ (eat) their dinner in silence. Later, the girl's father ¹¹ _____ (ask), 'Why did you want to know about spiders earlier?' She replied, 'Oh, there was a spider in your soup. But it ¹² _____ (go) now.'

4 ⭐⭐ Write questions with the present perfect or the past simple.
  1 a you / ever / tell / a lie? _Have you ever told a lie?_
    b Who / you / tell / the lie to?
       _____
    c Why / you / tell / it?
       _____
  2 a anyone / ever / tell / you a secret?
       _____
    b it / a very big secret?
       _____
    c you / ever / tell / another person the secret?
       _____

5 ⭐⭐⭐ Choose question 1 or 2 from Exercise 4. Write your answers.
  _____
  _____

WRITING
A listicle

1 ⭐ Read the listicle and (circle) the best title.
1. How to communicate with people from other countries
2. How to be a good language learner
3. How to be a better communicator
4. How to tell jokes

Over the last few years, I've learned a few things and now I can communicate much better than before. Here are my top five tips.

- **Use body language**
Use your hands and gesture to make a point, and always make eye contact. Since I started doing this, people have paid a lot more attention to me!

- **Use intonation**
Your tone of voice, that is how it sounds, shows your feelings. If your voice sounds flat and bored, your listener will be bored, too! Before, I didn't use to think about intonation, but now I understand that how you say something is very important.

- **Be a good listener**
Good communicators listen. Of course, say what you want to say, but later on, ask questions to find out what the other person is thinking.

- **Be yourself!**
Most people can tell when someone is telling a lie. All my life, I've never been very confident or sociable. Be honest and don't try to appear more confident than you really are. Always be yourself.

- **Tell jokes**
Smile and try to find the funny side whenever you can – this will make your listener more relaxed. This is especially important these days, when the world can be such a serious place.

Try to use some of these helpful tips and you'll soon be able to see the difference it makes!

2 ⭐⭐ Read the listicle again and complete the sentences.
1. People pay more attention to you when you _use your hands and gesture, and make eye contact._
2. _____ lets the listener know how you are feeling.
3. Good communicators listen and _____.
4. It's a bad idea to not tell the truth when you meet people because _____.
5. Telling jokes helps the listener to be _____.

3 ⭐⭐ (Circle) the correct meanings for the *Useful language* words and phrases.
1. **over the last few years** (recently) / since I was a baby
2. **since** at the moment / from a specific time in the past
3. **before** earlier / after some time has passed
4. **later on** after some time has passed / recently
5. **all my life** since I was born / at the moment
6. **these days** at the moment / earlier
7. **soon** earlier / in the very near future

Write your own listicle.

PLAN

4 ⭐⭐ Choose one of the other titles from Exercise 1 for your listicle and write some notes.

> Title
> Introduction
> A list of five tips
> A short ending

WRITE

5 ⭐⭐⭐ Write your listicle. Remember to include an introduction, five tips and a short ending, *can, could, will be able to* and the correct past tenses, and *Useful language* words and phrases.

CHECK

6 Do you …
- have an interesting title to interest the reader?
- have an ending to make the reader think?

3 REVIEW

VOCABULARY

1 Circle the correct words.

People ¹*greet / gesture* each other in many ways when they meet. All around the world, it's very common to ²*whisper / wave* when you want to attract someone's attention, and then simply ³*smile / shout* to show that you are happy. If we don't do this, then the other person might ⁴*interpret / translate* your serious face as meaning that you don't want to meet them. Perhaps the most common way to say hello in Europe and North America is to ⁵*wave / shake* hands. In other places, like Japan, people bow (move their head and body forwards). In the Philippines, some people perform a ⁶*gesture / shake* called mano (this Spanish word ⁷*posts / translates* as 'hand' into English), putting the other person's hand on their head. In some cultures, people put their noses together when they meet. In Costa Rica, however, people ⁸*shout / whisper* 'Ooooooooopppe!' in a very loud voice when they meet!

2 Complete the sentences with the correct form of *say* or *tell*.
1. Can I _____ you a secret?
2. I'd like to know how to _____ 'I love you' in Italian.
3. When you don't want to do something, you can always _____ no.
4. I know I said I was 16, but I wasn't _____ the truth.
5. Paula didn't _____ hello to me at the party.
6. George _____ me the story of how his parents met. It was really funny.
7. I'm not very good at _____ lies – my face always goes red!
8. Mike _____ a really terrible joke and no one laughed.

LANGUAGE IN ACTION

3 Tick (✓) the correct sentences and correct five incorrect sentences
1. I can swim when I was only two years old. ☐
2. I think I can to be able to get a good job in the future. ☐
3. I couldn't come to the party last night because I was ill. ☐
4. Will you be able to phone me when you get home? ☐
5. I can't speak English until I went to school. ☐
6. Can you watch TV late at night at the weekend? ☐
7. The school will be able let me know about my exam results next week. ☐
8. Now I could speak Italian well, but in the past I couldn't. ☐

30 SPREAD THE WORD! | UNIT 3

4 **Complete the sentences with the past simple or present perfect form of the verbs in brackets.**
1 I _____ (live) in London for about ten years – I love it here.
2 Before you came to London, how long _____ (you / live) in New York?
3 It _____ (be) 50 years since the first man stepped on the Moon.
4 They _____ (not learn) much Russian in Moscow – they were only there for two months.
5 My sister _____ (not finish) reading that book, but she will soon.
6 I _____ (not do) any exercise last week, so I want to do lots this week.
7 You and Frank get on really well. How long _____ (you / know) him?
8 I can't play football this afternoon because I _____ (fall) off my bike yesterday.

CUMULATIVE LANGUAGE

5 **Complete the text with the missing words. (Circle) the correct options.**

¹_____ heard the story *The Boy Who Cried Wolf*? The parents of a young boy asked him to look after their sheep on a lonely mountain. The boy ²_____ yes, but he soon found that it was a very boring job. After about four hours, he decided to do something interesting. He started shouting, 'Help! Wolf!' There ³_____ no wolf, of course, but his parents came running.
'Where's the wolf?' they asked.
'Sorry!' said the boy, 'I ⁴_____.'
The parents ⁵_____ very angry and went back to the village. A few hours ⁶_____ when suddenly the boy saw a real wolf! 'Help! Wolf!' he shouted. But this time, no one came. They thought it was a joke again! This ⁷_____ an old story, but the message is still relevant. For example, once I ⁸_____ to go to school, so I told my parents I was ill. I don't ⁹_____ tell lies, so they believed me and I didn't go to school that day. But unfortunately, the next week, I really was ill. My parents didn't believe me this time and I ¹⁰_____ stay at home – I felt terrible! I ¹¹_____ lied since then! So remember: don't tell lies, because one day you ¹²_____ cry wolf when you really need to!

	a	b	c
1	Have you ever	Have ever you	Haven't you never
2	is saying	said	told
3	is	were	was
4	was joking	joke	have joked
5	was	were	have been
6	are passing	have passed	passed
7	has been	is being	is
8	didn't want	didn't wanted	couldn't want
9	usually	never	sometimes
10	won't be able	couldn't	can't
11	don't	didn't	haven't
12	can't	couldn't	won't be able to

4 HEALTHY BODY, HEALTHY MIND

VOCABULARY
Health and fitness

1 ★ Complete the words and phrases with the vowels (a, e, i, o, u).

1 sw_e_ _a_t
2 c_ _gh
3 r_l_x
4 tr_ _n
5 sn_ _z_
6 g_t b_tt_r
7 g_ j_gg_ng
8 h_v_ _ f_v_r
9 g_t _ll
10 g_t str_ss_d
11 w_rm _p
12 w_rk _ _t
13 g_t _n_ _gh sl_ _p

2 ★ Tick (✓) the words or phrases which are in the correct column and put a cross (✗) next to the words in the incorrect column. Then write one extra word for each column.

HEALTH		FITNESS	
1 cough	✓	7 go jogging	☐
2 get better	☐	8 have a fever	☐
3 work out	☐	9 train	☐
4 relax	☐	10 sneeze	☐
5 warm up	☐	11 get enough sleep	☐
6 _____		12 _____	

3 ★★ Complete the sentences with the correct form of the words from Exercise 1.

1 Is it true that you can't _sneeze_ with your eyes open?
2 Sam is _____ for a half marathon at the moment.
3 A Isabel can't come today. She's not feeling very well.
   B Oh, no! I hope she _____ soon!
4 He _____ a lot when he exercises. His clothes get very wet!
5 Remember to _____ before you run or do exercise, especially in cold weather.
6 Don't _____ about your exams – relax, you'll be OK!

4 ★★ Circle the correct options.

CARO Hey, Azra! Do you want to go ¹*jogging* / *sweating* in the park? Meet me there?

AZRA Sorry, I can't. I'm getting ²*better* / *stressed* about my exams.

CARO Oh, come on! Working ³*out* / *in* will be good for you!

AZRA I have a ⁴*sneeze* / *fever* too. I'm really hot and I feel terrible.

CARO Oh, no! But it isn't a good idea to do school work if you want to get ⁵*better* / *stressed*.

AZRA I know … anyway, you're ⁶*training* / *relaxing* for the marathon – it's very difficult to run with you! 🙁

CARO OK. Get enough ⁷*exercise* / *sleep*. Don't study all night!

AZRA OK, and don't forget to ⁸*work out* / *warm up* before running. You hurt your leg last time!

Explore it!

Guess the correct answer.
Almost half of all the bones in the human body are in the *hands and feet* / *legs and arms* / *head and back*.

Find an interesting fact about exercise and the human body and send the question in an email to a classmate or ask them in the next class.

READING
Online FAQs

1 ★ Match the photos (a–d) with the FAQs and answers (1–4).

Home   News   **FAQs**

Read some of our FAQs about keeping fit and healthy during the school week and study sessions.

1 **Q** What can I do to get active during a school day and when can I do it?
A Getting exercise on a school day can be easy. Not enough people cycle or walk to and from school. And if that takes too much of your time, then use your lunch break to exercise or join a sports club after school.

2 **Q** I spend too much time sitting at a desk and not enough time on my feet. What can I do?
A We spend too many hours sitting at a desk or in front of a **screen**. Standing up exercises many different **muscles**. These muscles can become **weak** when we don't use them enough. You can now buy **adjustable** desks, which you can make higher so you can stand up while working. It's a good idea to stand and walk around every half an hour during long study sessions.

3 **Q** What are fitness balls and how can they help me?
A Some people say they feel too silly sitting on a big plastic ball. But fitness balls are a great way to work out, as they help to build the muscles in your **back** and **stomach** … all while you're sitting down! A fitness ball for home study is perfect for long hours sitting at a desk.

4 **Q** There is too much noise and stress in my life. How can I get a little quiet time?
A One word: yoga. The practice of yoga is hundreds of years old and when you find a little time between studying and exams to relax in this way, you can concentrate better. It's free and it's easy to do alone!

GET MORE INFORMATION HERE

2 ★★ Match the words in bold in the online FAQs with the meanings.
1 you need these to carry heavy objects _muscles_
2 the opposite of strong _____
3 where food goes in the body _____
4 the part of a computer where you see words or pictures _____
5 if something is this, you can change it to make it better. _____
6 the part of the body which is opposite to the front _____

3 ★★ Read the online FAQs again and answer the questions.
1 What times of the day can students do exercise, according to the FAQs?
   Before and after school and at lunchtime.
2 What can happen to the body when we don't stand up regularly?
   _____
3 How often do you need to move around when studying?
   _____
4 Why is the fitness ball unpopular with some people?
   _____
5 How can a fitness ball help your body?
   _____
6 Which activity can students do to relax, according to the FAQs?
   _____

4 ★★★ Answer the questions.
1 Which of the things in the FAQs have you tried?
   _____
2 Think of one more FAQ about young people's health and fitness.
   _____

UNIT 4 | HEALTHY BODY, HEALTHY MIND 33

LANGUAGE IN ACTION
Quantifiers

1 ★ Complete the sentences with *much* or *many*.
1. Kylie did too __much__ exercise yesterday and now she's very tired.
2. Is it possible to have too _____ fun at the weekend?
3. There were too _____ people in the pool, so we didn't swim.
4. Everyone I know has too _____ work to take winter holidays.
5. Skiing costs too _____ money for most students.
6. Too _____ students get stressed at exam time.

2 ★ Match the beginnings of the sentences (1–6) with the ends (a–f).
1. Swimming is great, but only a few [c]
2. Please give me a little more [ ]
3. Relaxing is hard: I need a little [ ]
4. Our nearest gym is a few [ ]
5. It's very hot, so take a little [ ]
6. Stand up for just a few [ ]

a. minutes every half an hour.
b. kilometres away.
c. schools have got swimming pools.
d. water with you.
e. help from my yoga teacher.
f. time to finish my homework.

3 ★★ Put the words in the correct order to make sentences.
1. long / school / aren't / enough / days / Normal
   Normal school days aren't long enough.
2. noisy / My / too / friend's / are / dogs
   _____
3. enough / I'm / drive / can't / not / because / I / old
   _____
4. her / Nasrin / desk / too / says / low / is
   _____
5. everyone / aren't / chairs / for / There / enough
   _____

4 ★★ Match the meanings (a–e) with the sentences (1–5) in Exercise 3.
a. He/She's too young. [3]
b. They're too short. [ ]
c. They're not quiet enough. [ ]
d. It's not high enough. [ ]
e. There are too many people. [ ]

5 ★★★ Complete the online post and its response with the phrases in the box.

> a few problems   enough strength
> not enough answers   not enough options
> ~~too many questions~~   too old   too young (x2)

Young Teen Health   FORUM
Posts:

I'd like to see more advice about health and fitness for boys on this website. There are ¹ _too many questions_ from teenage girls and ² _____ for boys. What advice can you give young male teens for a regular work out?
Ahmet

Thanks for your comment, Ahmet! Teenage boys can also have ³ _____ with their body image as they are growing up and changing. Fitness for boys is easy when you're young, but the early teenage years can be complicated. You feel you're ⁴ _____ to play silly games with friends but ⁵ _____ to work out in the gym with older guys. Perhaps you haven't got ⁶ _____ yet to join an adult sports team. But you're never ⁷ _____ to exercise regularly. If there are ⁸ _____ where you live, think about running or parkour, or working out at home. Hope this helps!

34 HEALTHY BODY, HEALTHY MIND | UNIT 4

VOCABULARY AND LISTENING
Healthy eating
An interview

1 ⭐ Complete the puzzle. Use the clues.

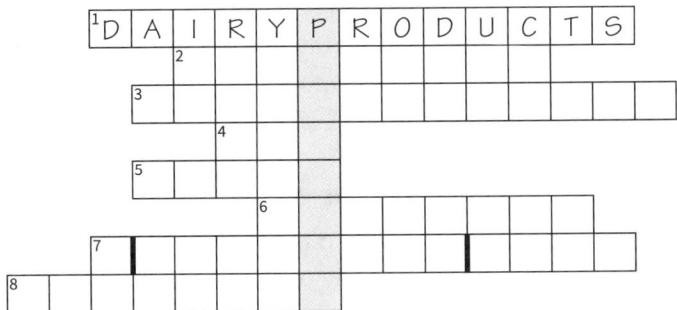

1 These foods usually come from milk.
2 You can study this to learn about food and a healthy diet.
3 We get most of our energy from these. You find them in bread and pasta.
4 There is a lot of this in cheese and chocolate.
5 This helps food pass through the body.
6 We get these natural substances from fruit (C) or sunlight (D).
7 A good mixture of many food types.
8 We count these to find out how much energy there is in our food.

2 ⭐ (Circle) the correct definition for the secret word (in grey) in Exercise 1.
a They help your bones to grow longer.
b They help your body to grow stronger.
c They help your heart to work.

3 🎧 4.01 ⭐⭐ Underline the words that are the same or similar in your language – notice any differences in spelling. Then listen to the English pronunciation.
1 A balance between mental and physical health is important.
2 We know that calcium is good for our bones.
3 Do you know why cereals are good for you?
4 Our sports lessons always end with a fun activity.

4 🎧 4.02 ⭐⭐ Listen to an interview about 'Blue Zones'. Number the topics the speakers mention in the order you hear them (1–4).
a ☐ regular exercise
b ☐ the Mediterranean diet
c ☐ 1 centenarians
d ☐ eating food from the sea

5 🎧 4.02 ⭐⭐ Listen again and (circle) the correct answers.
1 A Blue Zone is a place where people often …
   a become large.   b live to an old age.
   c eat seafood.
2 Philippa was surprised because many Blue Zones are …
   a very big.   b in Asia.   c islands.
3 The food tofu is very high in …
   a carbohydrates.   b calories.   c protein.
4 Philippa says people in the Mediterranean often eat …
   a too much meat.   b very little fat.
   c a lot of sweet things.
5 Philippa thinks that … also important for a long life.
   a family and friends are   b working outside is
   c getting up early is

UNIT 4 | HEALTHY BODY, HEALTHY MIND 35

LANGUAGE IN ACTION
should, shouldn't and *ought to*

1 ⭐ Look at the photos. Complete the sentences with *should* or *shouldn't* and the correct verb.

 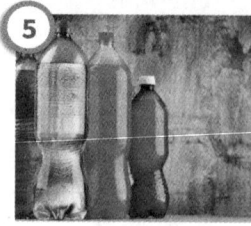 

1 You __should eat__ enough fruit.
2 You _____ too much coffee.
3 You _____ too much chocolate.
4 You _____ enough fish.
5 You _____ too many sweet drinks.
6 You _____ enough vegetables.

2 ⭐⭐ Complete the sentences with *should*, *shouldn't* or *ought*.

1 If you're always late for class, you __should__ get up earlier.
2 People who can't get up _____ go to bed so late.
3 Ilona can't relax: I think she _____ to do yoga.
4 Our teacher said we _____ to eat our lunch outside because it's hot today.
5 You _____ give chocolate to dogs – it's bad for them.
6 We _____ eat more tofu because it's full of protein.

3 ⭐⭐ <u>Underline</u> and correct one mistake in each sentence.

1 You don't look well; perhaps you <u>shouldn't</u> see a doctor. __should__
2 Our fridge is empty so we ought go to the shops. _____
3 You should worry so much about your exams. _____
4 What should I to do to get fitter? _____
5 He oughts to eat more protein. _____
6 You shouldn't to eat unhealthy food if you want to live to be 100. _____

4 ⭐⭐⭐ Complete the web article with the phrases in the box.

> ought to check   ~~ought to know~~
> ought to start   should drink   should be
> should take   shouldn't carry
> shouldn't spend

Top tips for a road trip – by bike!

Planning a road trip by bike? Here's what you ¹ _ought to know_ to stay fit and healthy!

Your bike ² _____ light enough because if it's too heavy, cycling becomes difficult in hot weather. But you ³ _____ that it's big enough for you – a bike that's too small soon gets uncomfortable.

You ⁴ _____ too many things with you. Too many bags slow you down, so you ⁵ _____ two small bags, maximum. You ⁶ _____ lots of water, so take a one-litre water bottle.

You ⁷ _____ too much money on maps: paper maps are heavy. Download maps onto your smartphone before you leave home. And finally, you ⁸ _____ early in the day – before it gets too hot!

5 ⭐⭐⭐ Choose one of the topics in the box and write three pieces of advice. Use *should / ought to* and *shouldn't*.

> eating more healthily
> preparing for an exam
> writing an essay

1 _____
2 _____
3 _____

WRITING
A post on a forum

1  Read the post on a forum and the response. Who does Carlos want to help? What does Tom suggest?

_____

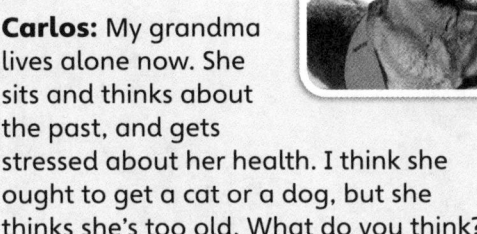

Forum:
All things animals
Posts:

Carlos: My grandma lives alone now. She sits and thinks about the past, and gets stressed about her health. I think she ought to get a cat or a dog, but she thinks she's too old. What do you think?

Tom@the Den: Hey, great that you've written to me – thanks! We all have stress in our lives and especially old people living alone. Pets make people feel happier and more relaxed. In fact, did you know that they can also help with stress? Have you ever tried sitting with a cat or walking a dog when you're stressed? It really helps! Why? Stress often causes high blood pressure and just being near an animal can help to lower it. I think your grandma should definitely try having a pet. If she likes dogs, for example, but doesn't want to keep a dog as a pet, I can recommend trying a therapy dog. There are specially trained dogs that can visit old people with their owners or volunteers. Your grandma can enjoy the dog without worrying about it! Why don't you look online for a therapy pet centre near you? Or you could always ask at your local vets – they ought to be able to help. That way, your grandma can relax and beat stress.

2 ★★ Read the post and response again. Answer the questions.
1 Why doesn't Carlos's grandma want a pet?
   She thinks she's too old.
2 How can pets help with stress?
   _____
3 Where should Carlos find out about a therapy pet?
   _____
4 Why is a therapy pet a better option for Carlos's grandma?
   _____

3 ★★ (Circle) the correct options in the *Useful language* phrases. Then check in the forum response.
1 You *would* / *could* always ask …
2 Have you ever tried *sitting* / *sit* … ?
3 *This* / *That* way, your grandma can relax …
4 Why *don't* / *not* you look … ?
5 I can recommend *to try* / *trying* …

Write your own response to a post on a forum.

PLAN

4 ★★ Write notes on the problem below or use your own ideas. Include a greeting, thanks, advice and reasons for your advice.

> 'Please help! I'm drinking two litres of cola a day! I know it's bad for me, but I think I'm addicted to the sugar and caffeine! What can I do?'

WRITE

5 ★★★ Write your response. Remember to use *should*, *shouldn't*, *ought to*, quantifiers and *Useful language* phrases.

CHECK

6 Do you …
- have a greeting?
- give advice with reasons?
- use an informal style?

4 REVIEW

VOCABULARY

1 Look at the photos and circle the correct options.

2 Match the beginnings of the sentences (1–8) with the ends (a–h).

1 **Nutrition** is the food we eat ☐
2 Hamburgers, ice cream and chocolate ☐
3 The number of **calories** in food ☐
4 **Carbohydrates** give us ☐
5 **Protein** helps our bodies ☐
6 Fruit and vegetables contain ☐
7 A **balanced diet** ☐
8 Lots of **fibre** is good for the stomach ☐

a tells us how much energy it has.
b to grow and be healthy and strong.
c a lot of **vitamins** A and C.
d and how our body uses it.
e the energy we need to move.
f have a lot of **fat** in them.
g and travels through the body quickly.
h is eating a good variety of healthy food.

LANGUAGE IN ACTION

3 Circle the correct options.
1 Is there *little / enough* food for everyone or should I cook more?
2 We don't use too *many / much* milk products in our restaurant.
3 Owen's just gone out to buy *a few / a little* eggs.
4 We all need to relax and have *much / a little* fun.
5 My baby sister isn't *old enough / enough old* to make her own breakfast.
6 This article gives you *a little / few* ideas on healthy diets.

1 *sneeze / cough*

5 *warm up / sweat*

2 *sneeze / cough*

6 *have a fever / get enough sleep*

3 *go jogging / warm up*

7 *sweat / warm up*

4 *relax / get ill*

8 *get stressed / get enough sleep*

38 HEALTHY BODY, HEALTHY MIND | UNIT 4

4 Complete the sentences with *should*, *shouldn't* or *ought*.

1 What _____ we eat to grow stronger?
2 The children _____ to eat fewer crisps and sweets.
3 A balanced diet _____ to have a little of everything.
4 You _____ drink coffee at night – it stops you from sleeping.
5 How much exercise _____ we do?
6 You _____ eat more than you need.

CUMULATIVE LANGUAGE

5 Complete the conversation with the missing words. Circle the correct options.

INTERVIEWER You've just completed a marathon, well done! I'm sure you're tired, but ¹_____ to answer a few questions?
BERNADETTE Sure, I just need ²_____ water. OK, so yeah, it was a great run.
INTERVIEWER It was! You ³_____ a runner, did you? Tell us how it started.
BERNADETTE I often got ill when I was younger and I wasn't ⁴_____ to do sport.
INTERVIEWER That's hard to believe! You've ⁵_____ a marathon in record time!
BERNADETTE As a child I spent ⁶_____ time in bed and I really wasn't fit at all.
INTERVIEWER Not enough young people exercise as much as they ⁷_____ to. What changed for you?
BERNADETTE One day, my mother ⁸_____ a TV programme about foods that some people ⁹_____ eat because it makes them ill. We later discovered that I ¹⁰_____ eat bread or anything with gluten in it.
INTERVIEWER And what ¹¹_____ then?
BERNADETTE I changed my diet right then and I ¹²_____ gluten since then. I felt better, started doing sport and the rest is history!

1 a can you   b will you be able   c should you
2 a too much   b a few   c a little
3 a didn't use to be   b used not to be   c didn't used to be
4 a enough strong   b too strong   c strong enough
5 a just completed   b still completed   c yet completed
6 a enough   b too little   c too much
7 a should   b ought   c shouldn't
8 a is seeing   b has seen   c saw
9 a can't   b can't to   c can
10 a shouldn't to   b shouldn't   c ought to
11 a happens   b happen   c happened
12 a didn't eat   b haven't eaten   c still didn't eat

5 SAVE OUR PLANET!

VOCABULARY
Planet Earth

1 ⭐ **Complete the crossword. Use the clues.**

DOWN ↓

1 We usually separate our paper, plastic and food ... into different bins.
2 I try to save ... at home – I always turn off the lights when I'm not using them.
3 Cycling or walking is better for the ... than travelling by car.
5 Governments want to reduce the carbon ... (or CO₂) that their countries produce.
8 We all live on the ... Earth.

ACROSS →

4 Tigers are an ... species. It's possible they will all die in a few years.
6 There used to be a lot of ... near here, like birds and butterflies, but not now.
7 Trees produce ... for us to breathe.
8 Traffic causes a lot of air ... in cities.
9 ... change causes hotter weather around the world.
10 ... power from the sun produces a lot of electricity in hot countries.
11 Plastic in the sea is bad for all ... life, from large whales to small fish.

Explore it!

Guess the correct answer.
How much of the plastic that we use every year ends up in the seas and oceans?
a 1%   b 5%   c 10%

Find an interesting fact about pollution in the sea and send the question in an email to a classmate or ask them in the next class.

2 ⭐⭐ **Complete the notes with words from Exercise 1.**

Things we should reduce
• the amount of carbon ¹ _dioxide_ that we produce
• ² _____ (e.g. air, water and noise – less traffic!)
• ³ _____ (e.g. plastic and food)
• the effects of ⁴ _____ (e.g. rising temperatures and seas)
• the amount of ⁵ _____ that we use (e.g. electricity and gas)

Things we need to protect or save
• the ⁶ _____ (the air, our water, etc.)
• ⁷ _____ (e.g. fish and other sea animals)
• the ⁸ _____ Earth (our home – we only have one!)
• all animals, but especially ⁹ _____ (e.g. tigers and gorillas)

3 ⭐⭐⭐ **Circle the correct words.**

We face many environmental problems, such as rising levels of ¹(carbon) / oxygen dioxide in the air, which cause ²climate / planet change. Plastic is also a big cause of ³pollution / waste. Every year, we put lots of plastic ⁴energy / waste into our seas and oceans. This is a huge problem for ⁵endangered / marine life. It ends up in the stomachs of fish, which bigger animals then eat, including us. Many animals are therefore becoming ⁶endangered / marine. But plastic gets everywhere on the ⁷planet / environment. Even high mountains now have millions of tiny pieces of plastic on them, carried there by the wind.

READING
A news story

1 ⭐ Look at the photos and read the news story quickly. (Circle) the best title.

a Why we should use drinking straws
b The history of drinking straws
c The end of drinking straws?

2 ⭐⭐ Complete the article with the missing sentence parts (a–f).

a end up in the seas and oceans, as waste
b such as bags, cups or bottles
c ~~they can be fun to drink with~~
d people are starting to do something about the problem
e including when we haven't asked for one
f has decided not to have plastic straws in any of her houses

3 ⭐⭐ Match the words in bold in the news story with the definitions.

1 things on a list _items_
2 put something in the bin after we have used it _____
3 an official law that stops something from happening _____
4 use something again, or change it into something different _____
5 small bits of rubbish in public places _____

Most of us have used straws. They are useful and ¹ _they can be fun to drink with_. When we get a cola or juice from a café or restaurant, for example, it often comes with a straw, ² _____. We usually use them once and then **dispose** of them immediately. In fact, people in the USA use 500 million every day. That's enough straws to go around the planet 2.5 times!

The big problem with straws is that many of them ³ _____. Europeans **recycle** only about 30% of their plastic, and straws are in the top ten i**tems** of **litter** found on beaches every year.

The good news is that ⁴ _____. More and more big companies are deciding not to use straws, or to provide them only when customers have asked for them. The US city of Seattle has already put a **ban** on straws, and the European Union wants to do the same by 2030. Scotland plans to do this in 2019. Even the British Queen ⁵ _____.

So, it is possible that plastic drinking straws will soon be a thing of the past. Many people believe that we can continue to protect our environment by also reducing all the other plastic objects that we only use once, ⁶ _____.

4 ⭐⭐ What do these numbers in the news story describe?

1 30 _The amount of their plastic, in percent, that Europeans recycle._
2 500 million _____
3 2.5 _____
4 2019 _____
5 10 _____

5 ⭐⭐⭐ Apart from a ban, how can we reduce the number of plastic straws people use? Write three ideas.

_____
_____
_____

UNIT 5 | SAVE OUR PLANET! 41

LANGUAGE IN ACTION
The first conditional

1 ⭐ Circle the correct options.
1. If I *see* / *don't see* any litter on the beach, I'll pick it up.
2. I won't use my bike tomorrow *unless* / *if* it's raining. I don't want to get wet.
3. Unless we *use* / *don't use* alternative forms of energy, we will create more air pollution.
4. If you *will leave* / *leave* your computer on all night, it will waste energy.
5. Some cities *may* / *may be* under water if sea levels rise.
6. I'll travel by train if I *go* / *might go* on holiday this year.

2 ⭐⭐ Complete the sentences with the phrases in the box.

> climate change may get worse
> if we stop using so much plastic
> ~~it will help the planet~~
> many types of plant will be in danger
> there might be more plastic than fish by 2050
> unless we protect them

1. If we reduce our energy use,
   it will help the planet.
2. Many animals could become endangered
   _____.
3. If we lose lots of insect species,
   _____.
4. If we don't reduce the amount of carbon dioxide,
   _____.
5. Unless we stop polluting our oceans,
   _____.
6. It will help the planet
   _____.

3 ⭐⭐ Complete the text with the verbs in the box.

> act   continue   is   might be
> ~~might not see~~   will need

If you drive somewhere on a summer's night and check the front window of your car after, you ¹ *might not see* many dead insects on it. This doesn't sound like a problem. In fact, if your car ² _____ clean, you will probably be pleased. However, this is a worrying sign. Over the last 30 years, numbers of insects have fallen by 75%. But if there are fewer flies and mosquitoes in the future, the world ³ _____ a better place, right? Wrong! The problem is that if insects ⁴ _____ to disappear, we will all be in trouble. Many plants depend on them. As insects move from one plant to another, they carry pollen, which helps plants to grow again. And if the number of people on the planet keeps on rising, we ⁵ _____ more and more food. Unless we ⁶ _____ quickly, insect numbers could fall even more. This could be very bad news for both humans and the planet.

4 ⭐⭐⭐ Rewrite the second sentence so that it has a similar meaning to the first. Use the words in brackets.
1. If we don't do something soon, it's possible that endangered species will disappear.
   Endangered species could disappear if we don't do something soon. (could)
2. There will be huge problems if we don't protect our environment.
   _____ our environment, there will be huge problems. (unless)
3. If we don't stop using chemicals on farms, it's possible that insect numbers will fall.
   _____ if we don't stop using chemicals on farms. (might)
4. If we do something now, we might stop climate change.
   Unless we do something now, we _____ climate change. (might)

5 ⭐⭐⭐ Complete the sentences with your own ideas.
1. Unless we do something about climate change, _____.
2. We might be able to help the planet if _____.

VOCABULARY AND LISTENING
Natural environments

1 ⭐ Look at the photos and complete the natural environment words.

1 b_ay_ 2 v_____ 3 c_____ 4 c_____ 5 c_____

6 i_____ 7 r_____ 8 s_____ 9 v_____ 10 w_____

2 ⭐ Choose the three most difficult words to remember from Exercise 1. Then draw a picture of each one in your notebook (see the *Learn to learn* tip in the Student's Book, p65).

3 ⭐⭐ (Circle) the correct options.
1 A *stream* / *bay* is a small river, usually in the countryside.
2 You only find *icebergs* / *cliffs* in very cold places like the Arctic.
3 A *valley* / *cave* is a big hole in a mountain or under the ground.
4 A *cliff* / *valley* is a high area of vertical rock, usually near the sea.
5 A *stream* / *waterfall* is where a river falls from a high point to a lower point.
6 A *volcano* / *bay* is a mountain with a hole at the top. Sometimes gases and hot liquids come out.
7 A *rainforest* / *waterfall* is a hot place with trees and lots of animals.
8 A *bay* / *valley* is an area between hills or mountains. There is often a river at the bottom.

A class discussion

🎧 4 ⭐ Listen to the class discussion. Which four natural environments from Exercise 1 do the students mention?
5.01
_____

🎧 5 ⭐⭐ Listen again and complete the notes.
5.01

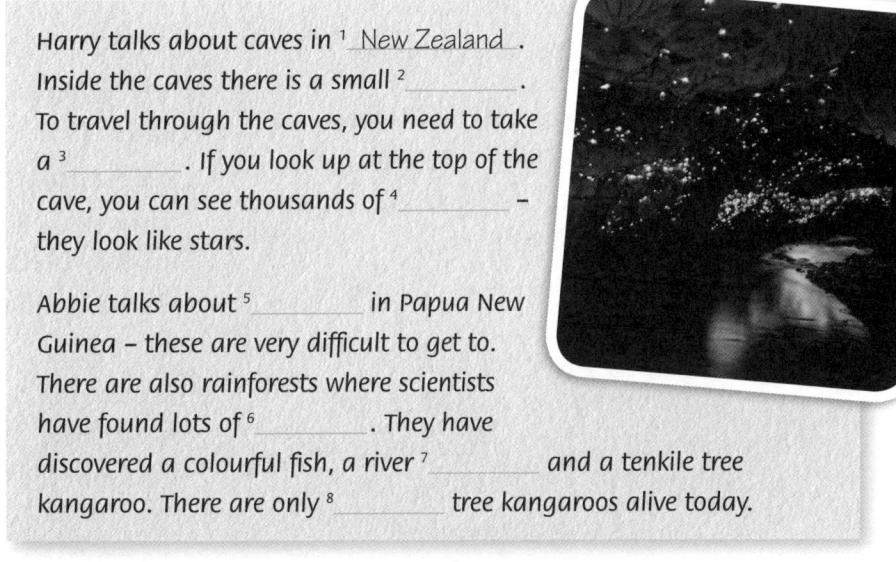

Harry talks about caves in ¹ _New Zealand_. Inside the caves there is a small ² _____. To travel through the caves, you need to take a ³ _____. If you look up at the top of the cave, you can see thousands of ⁴ _____ – they look like stars.

Abbie talks about ⁵ _____ in Papua New Guinea – these are very difficult to get to. There are also rainforests where scientists have found lots of ⁶ _____. They have discovered a colourful fish, a river ⁷ _____ and a tenkile tree kangaroo. There are only ⁸ _____ tree kangaroos alive today.

6 ⭐⭐⭐ Think of three examples of natural environments from Exercise 1 in your country. What are their names?
_____
_____

UNIT 5 | SAVE OUR PLANET! 43

LANGUAGE IN ACTION
The second conditional

1 ⭐ Circle the correct options.
1 If I could travel anywhere in the world, …
   a I'll visit a jungle.
   b I'd visit a jungle.
   c I visited a jungle.

2 I don't know what would happen …
   a if all the insects will disappear.
   b if all the insects would disappear.
   c if all the insects disappeared.

3 What would happen if …
   a we cut down all the rainforests?
   b we'd cut down all the rainforests?
   c would we cut down all the rainforests?

4 If I were you, …
   a I'd find out more information.
   b I found out more information.
   c I'm finding out more information.

5 People wouldn't buy plastic products …
   a if they have a better alternative.
   b if they had a better alternative.
   c if they'd have a better alternative.

2 ⭐⭐ Complete the second conditional sentences using the verbs in brackets.
1 If I _had_ a bike, I would _use_ it to go to school. (have / use)
2 I _____ out today if it _____ cold. (go / not be)
3 If they _____ near the sea, they _____ to the beach a lot. (live / go)
4 The waterfall _____ more interesting to look at if it _____ raining. (be / be)
5 If we _____ so much meat, we _____ so many rainforests. (not eat / not cut down)
6 Houses near the coast _____ in danger if sea levels _____ higher. (be / get)

3 ⭐⭐ Complete the blog post with the correct form of the verbs in the box to make second conditional sentences.

> be (x3)   ~~can~~   check   find
> not continue   not use   ~~try~~

HOME | ABOUT ME | ARCHIVE | FOLLOW

If I ¹ _could_ do anything to help the planet, I ² _would try_ to stop people buying so many things with palm oil in them. If you ³ _____ the ingredients in the things you buy, you ⁴ _____ palm oil in many of them – from biscuits to toothpaste. It's a cheap form of oil, and our products ⁵ _____ more expensive if companies ⁶ _____ it.

The oil comes from trees which only grow in hot countries. This means that we need to cut down rainforests to grow them. This is a problem for the animals that live in rainforests, including the orangutan. If we ⁷ _____ to destroy their natural habitat, orangutans wouldn't be endangered. So, if there ⁸ _____ one useful thing everyone could do to protect the environment, it ⁹ _____ to buy things which don't contain palm oil.

4 ⭐⭐⭐ Write second conditional sentences about the situations.
1 People use so much plastic. There is so much waste.
   If people _didn't use so much plastic, there wouldn't be_ so much waste.
2 I haven't got a recycling bin, so I don't recycle my rubbish.
   If I _____ my rubbish.
3 People don't know about palm oil, so they buy products which use it.
   If people _____ products which use it.
4 We don't use solar power in our country. There isn't enough sunlight.
   If _____ solar power in our country.
5 Palm oil is cheap. That's why companies use it.
   If palm oil _____ it.

44 SAVE OUR PLANET! | UNIT 5

WRITING
An opinion essay

1 ⭐ Read the essay. Which environmental problem in the photos (a–c) does the writer think is the most serious?

Our most serious environmental problem

There are many environmental problems nowadays and it is difficult to know which one is the most important. Some people ¹ _believe_ that we should protect the rainforests. Other people might think that we need to stop using plastic. Which is the most important?

It would be good if we could solve both of these problems. ² _____, in my ³ _____, the most serious problem is air pollution. This is something that is getting worse in cities around the world. ⁴ _____, it has an effect on everyone as it is a major cause of ill health, especially in children.

In my ⁵ _____, the first step would be to reduce the number of cars in cities, as this is one of the biggest causes of pollution. In ⁶ _____ to this, we need to make more people use public transport or cleaner forms of personal transport like bicycles. We also need cleaner factories that don't produce dangerous gases which are bad for our health.

To ⁷ _____ up, if we have cleaner cities with cleaner air, we will all become healthier. We will also spend more time outdoors, exercising and enjoying our natural environment.

2 ⭐⭐ Complete the essay with the words in the box. Sometimes more than one answer is possible.

> addition   ~~believe~~   Furthermore
> However   opinion   sum   view

3 ⭐⭐ (Circle) the correct options.
1 The first paragraph includes an introduction and *a question / the writer's main opinion*.
2 The second paragraph gives *the writer's main / other people's* opinion.
3 The third paragraph offers *reasons for / possible solutions to* the problem.
4 The last paragraph *introduces / summarises* the writer's opinion.

Write your own opinion essay.

PLAN

4 ⭐⭐ What do you think is the biggest environmental problem? Think of two ideas to support your opinion. Write notes.

Problem _____

Solution 1 _____

Solution 2 _____

5 Decide what information to include in each paragraph. Use the information in Exercise 3 to help you.

WRITE

6 Write your opinion essay. Remember to include four paragraphs, the first and second conditional, and words and phrases from the *Useful language* box (see Student's Book, p65).

CHECK

7 Do you …
- have an introduction with a question for the reader to think about?
- have ideas and examples to support your opinions?
- have a conclusion to support your opinion?

UNIT 5 | SAVE OUR PLANET! 45

5 REVIEW

VOCABULARY

1 Match the beginnings of the sentences (1–10) with the ends (a–j).

1. Too much carbon
2. It's important to save
3. Probably the biggest environmental problem is climate
4. We all need to recycle and reduce waste to help protect the
5. Plastic is a big problem for marine
6. Plants produce
7. The white rhino is an endangered
8. We all live on the same
9. Cars are the main cause of air
10. Sunny countries produce a lot of energy from

a change.
b species.
c oxygen, which all animals need to survive.
d planet, so we should look after it.
e life, like fish, whales and sea birds.
f dioxide causes global warming.
g pollution in cities.
h energy, and not waste it.
i solar power.
j environment.

2 Match the sentences with the words in the box.

> cave   cliff   coast   icebergs   rainforest
> stream   volcano   waterfall

1. We often have a picnic here. It's nice to sit by the water and see the ducks swimming past. _____
2. My grandparents have a house there. It's nice because you can just walk out onto the beach and you can hear the sea at night. _____
3. You can walk into it and it's really interesting. It's dark, but you can hear the sound of water deep below you. _____
4. Don't stand too near the edge. I know it's nice to look down at the sea, but it can be dangerous. _____
5. They cut down a large area, unfortunately, and it will take hundreds of years for the trees and plants to grow again. _____
6. They're very dangerous to boats and ships. Remember that you can only see 10% of them. The rest is below the sea. _____
7. Every second more than 150,000 gallons of water drops to the ground below at Niagara! _____
8. It's still active and you can often smell the gases – the heat and noise is incredible sometimes! _____

LANGUAGE IN ACTION

3 Tick (✓) the correct sentences and correct five incorrect sentences.

1. If I pass my exam tomorrow, I am really happy.
   _____
2. I might go for a walk along the coast tomorrow if the weather will be nice.
   _____
3. Will you call me if you're late?
   _____
4. Unless I don't do my homework now, I won't have time to go out later.
   _____
5. If I will have money, I will go to the cinema on Friday.
   _____
6. I won't buy a new phone unless this one breaks completely.
   _____
7. If you look in the stream, you will may see some fish.
   _____
8. You could have a rest if you feel tired.
   _____

46 SAVE OUR PLANET! | UNIT 5

4 Complete the sentences with the words in the box.

> didn't have   had   knew   took   was   were   would be
> would have   would need   would stop   would take   wouldn't be

1 If I _____ time, I _____ a trip to the bay.
2 The town _____ in trouble if that volcano _____ active.
3 If you _____ more sociable, you _____ more friends.
4 You _____ ill if you _____ better care of yourself.
5 If I _____ a bike, I _____ to use the bus.
6 More people _____ eating meat if they _____ about the effects on the environment.

CUMULATIVE LANGUAGE

5 Complete the text with the missing words. Circle the correct options.

I ¹_____ a TV documentary last month about marine life and plastic. Every day, we ²_____ lots of plastic waste in the oceans and even a little drinking straw can have a terrible effect on an animal. For example, if a fish ³_____ one, it could easily die. And if a sea bird ate the fish, it ⁴_____ the plastic, too. Plastic in the oceans is a big problem because it ⁵_____ away. It just breaks down into smaller and smaller pieces! ⁶_____ we do something about this problem, it will get worse. So, I ⁷_____ to make some changes to my life. They're small, but if everyone ⁸_____ something small, it would add up to something big. In the past, I ⁹_____ a lot of plastic straws and bags. I ¹⁰_____ straws without thinking about it in cafés. Now, I just say I don't need one when they offer. They haven't stopped using straws in cafés in my city ¹¹_____, but I hope they do soon. Anyway, we all need to do something. If we don't, then soon we ¹²_____ to enjoy the natural beauty of the sea and its marine life.

1 a have watched   b watched   c watch
2 a have put   b used to put   c put
3 a ate   b would eat   c will eat
4 a eats   b would eat   c will eat
5 a doesn't go   b wouldn't go   c isn't going
6 a If   b Furthermore   c Unless
7 a have decided   b am deciding   c will decide
8 a did   b does   c would do
9 a use to use   b used to use   c did use
10 a will use   b am using   c have used
11 a yet   b already   c since
12 a couldn't   b can't   c won't be able

6 THINK OUTSIDE THE BOX

VOCABULARY
Making things

1 ⭐ (Circle) 12 more verbs in the word snake.

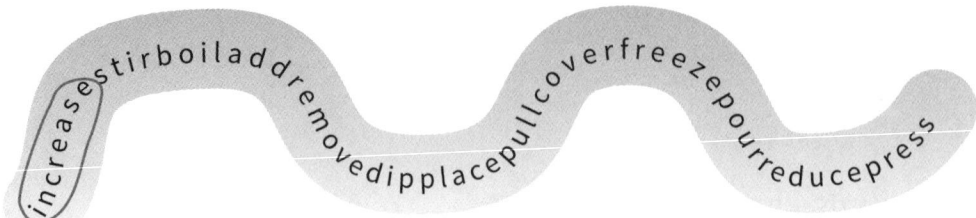

increase stir boil add remove dip place pull cover freeze pour reduce press

2 ⭐⭐ Complete the sentences with the correct form of the verbs from Exercise 1.

1. _Increase_ the oven temperature from 150 °C to 200 °C.
2. I want to _____ the time I spend watching TV from four hours to one hour a day.
3. Water _____ at 100 °C.
4. She _____ her feet in the sea for a few seconds – it was really cold!
5. _____ the hot water into the cup and _____ sugar and milk.
6. _____ the cake from the oven and _____ it on a plate to cool.
7. You should _____ the soup with a spoon so it doesn't burn and stick to the pan.
8. I _____ my eyes so I couldn't see the frightening scenes in the film.
9. Lara collects flowers – she _____ them flat and puts them in a scrapbook.
10. We use our car to _____ our caravan when we go on holiday.
11. You should _____ fresh fish at –20 °C for at least seven days before eating it.

3 ⭐ Choose one of the words from Exercise 1 and think of an image to go with it. Write your ideas in your notebook (see the *Learn to learn* tip in the Student's Book, p71).

4 ⭐⭐ (Circle) the correct words.
1. When the milk boils, (pour) / *pull* it into your coffee cup.
2. *Reduce* / *Increase* the temperature so that it's really cold.
3. Take a spoon and *remove* / *stir* the butter, sugar and milk together for a few minutes.
4. *Add* / *Cover* the glass with paper and put it in the fridge overnight.
5. I'll *freeze* / *press* any food that we don't eat and we can have it next month.
6. Don't *dip* / *freeze* your finger into the hot liquid!

Explore it!

Guess the correct answer.

A chef in the USA invented crisps when he …

a accidentally cooked some potatoes for too long.
b cut potatoes very thinly for an angry customer.
c poured hot fat over some frozen vegetables.

Find an interesting fact about an invention or discovery and send the question in an email to a classmate or ask them in the next class.

READING
A news story

1 ★★ Read the news story. Complete the paragraphs (A–D) with the headings (1–4).
   1 What was the problem?
   2 What was the solution?
   3 What do people use it for now?
   4 Who was Vesta Stoudt?

The story of duct tape

A _____

In the early 1940s, the US army was fighting in Europe in World War II. Vesta Stoudt was a woman from Illinois who had two sons in the military. As part of the war effort, she was working in a factory back home in the USA. Her job was to **inspect** and pack equipment for the soldiers in Europe.

B _____

At the factory, they closed and **secured** the boxes of equipment using a thin paper **tape**. However, the boxes were difficult to open quickly, especially when they were wet. Vesta was worried that soldiers' lives might be in danger because they might not be able to get their equipment out fast enough.

C _____

Vesta suggested that they closed the boxes with a stronger, **waterproof** tape. She designed a basic **prototype** of how she thought the tape should be. The boxes were easier to open quickly with this new tape. Vesta's managers in the factory didn't listen to her, but she didn't give up. She decided to write to Franklin Roosevelt, the president of the United States.

D _____

The letter worked and Vesta received a letter of thanks from Roosevelt. The government then asked a company to make the tape based on Vesta's idea. The tape was a great success and probably helped to save lives! Nowadays, duct tape, as it is known, is used for many different things and in many different industries. It is used by NASA in its spaceships and clothes are even made from it. And it's all thanks to the **patience** of one inspiring American woman.

2 ★★ Match the words in bold in the news story with the meanings.
   1 made safe from damage _secured_
   2 stopping liquid from entering somewhere _____
   3 the ability to stay calm and continue doing something difficult _____
   4 view closely to check condition _____
   5 a long, narrow piece of material we use to close things _____
   6 the first example of something _____

3 ★★ Read the new story again and answer the questions.
   1 Where did Vesta Stoudt work?
      In a factory in the USA.
   2 What did Vesta do at the factory?
      _____
   3 What problem did Vesta want to solve?
      _____
   4 Why was Vesta's prototype better than the paper tape?
      _____
   5 How did Vesta show patience?
      _____
   6 What examples does the writer give of how people use duct tape now?
      _____

4 ★★★ Can you think of any other ways people use duct tape? Write two ideas.

LANGUAGE IN ACTION
Present simple passive

1 ⭐ Complete the table with the past participle form of the verbs. Decide if the verb is regular or irregular.

Verb	Past participle	Regular	Irregular
add	added	✓	
break			
catch			
collect			
connect			
design			
develop			
eat			
manufacture			
throw			

2 ⭐⭐ Complete the sentences with the present simple passive form of the verbs in brackets.

1 How many mobile phones *are made* every year in Asia? (make)
2 Something new and exciting _____ every day. (invent)
3 The potatoes _____ in very hot oil to make crisps. (place)
4 These new inventions _____ enough, in my opinion. (not test)
5 _____ these materials _____ online or should we go to a shop? (sell)

3 ⭐⭐ Complete the sentences with the present simple passive form of verbs from Exercise 1.

1 Food waste *is collected* for recycling – what a great idea!
2 Sugar _____ to chocolate to make it sweet.
3 How many plastic bottles _____ in the rubbish bin every day?
4 New ideas _____ here by brilliant young inventors.
5 _____ your computer _____ to the Internet by a cable or wi-fi?
6 This system _____ to help blind people use a computer.

4 ⭐⭐ Write questions in the present simple passive. Then write the correct answers using the places in brackets.

1 coffee beans / grow / Iceland? (South America)
Are coffee beans grown in Iceland?
No, they aren't. Coffee beans are grown in South America.

2 most chocolate / produce / in Switzerland? (Germany)
_____

3 cars / manufacture / in Malta? (China)
_____

4 insects / eat / in the UK? (Thailand)
_____

5 bananas / grow / in Denmark? (Ecuador)
_____

5 ⭐⭐⭐ Complete the text with the present simple passive form of the verbs in brackets.

It's difficult to believe, but glass ¹ *is made* (make) of liquid sand. That's right, the same sand that ² _____ (find) on the beach or in the desert. When sand ³ _____ (heat) to about 1700 °C, it changes into a liquid. Other minerals ⁴ _____ (add) and when it cools to a much lower temperature, it changes into glass. To make glass containers, like jars or bottles, liquid glass ⁵ _____ (pour) into containers in a particular shape, called moulds. Of course, glass ⁶ _____ also _____ (use) for windows and we ⁷ _____ (protect) by glass, for example in cars, but glass breaks easily, too. Glass ⁸ _____ easily _____ (recycle), so manufacturers can often use the same glass again and again in their products.

VOCABULARY AND LISTENING
Materials and containers

1 ★ Match the materials with the containers in the box to make six objects. Then write the words in the correct column. Use each word only once.

> ~~bag~~ box can cardboard
> case glass jar leather
> rubber ~~silk~~ tin tube

Material	Container
¹ silk	bag
2	
3	
4	
5	
6	

2 ★★ Complete the sentences with the objects from Exercise 1.
1 Julia's dress hasn't got pockets. She needs a little ____silk bag____ to put her phone and purse in.
2 A garden hose is a _____. It's long and thin. You use it to put water on your flowers.
3 When Dad goes to work every morning, he carries his laptop and all his important papers in a _____.
4 Our new computer came in a big _____. We used it to put old books and clothes in.
5 Tuna, peas and beans – what other things come in a _____?
6 My grandma used to have a _____ full of sweets and chocolate for visiting children.

A conversation

3 ★ Look at the questions and think about possible answers.
1 What are jeans made of?
2 Who wears jeans?
3 How much do jeans cost?
4 What are the best styles?
5 What effect do jeans have on the environment?

🎧 4 ★ Listen to two friends shopping for jeans. Which three questions from Exercise 3 do the girls discuss?
6.01
_____

🎧 5 ★★ Listen again. Are the sentences T (true) or F (false)? Correct the false sentences.
6.01
1 Nicole prefers white jeans to blue jeans.
   F. Nicole prefers blue jeans.
2 The word 'denim' comes from the name of a French town.
_____
3 Camila says good jeans can cost about £100.
_____
4 Nicole says that some jeans factories use too much energy.
_____
5 Nicole says Camila should find out information before she buys jeans.
_____
6 Camila doesn't want to go to the shop that Nicole suggests.
_____

LANGUAGE IN ACTION
Past simple passive

1 ★ **Complete the sentences with the past simple passive form of the verbs in brackets.**

1 Tolstoy's novel *War and Peace* __was published__ (publish) in 1867.
2 The world's most expensive violins _____ (make) by Antonio Stradivari.
3 Facebook _____ (start) by Harvard University students in 2004.
4 Is it true that some of Shakespeare's plays _____ (not write) by him?
5 Lots of my photos _____ (lose) when my phone broke.
6 Paper _____ (not invent) in Europe but in China.

2 ★★ **Write questions in the past simple passive.**

1 when / first antibiotic / discover?
   When was the first antibiotic discovered?
2 where / the world's first underground railway / open?
   _____
3 where / the first modern Olympics / hold?
   _____
4 what / the first Pixar movie / call?
   _____
5 where / the largest Egyptian pyramids / build?
   _____
6 when / the first email / write?
   _____
7 where / the first CD / make?
   _____
8 when / Google / start?
   _____

3 ★★ **Match the answers in the box with the questions in Exercise 2. Write sentences in the past simple passive.**

| ~~1928~~ | 1971 | 1998 | Athens | Germany |
| Giza | *Toy Story* | London | | |

1 The first antibiotic was discovered in 1928.
2 _____
3 _____
4 _____
5 _____
6 _____
7 _____
8 _____

4 ★★★ **Read the text about Stonehenge. Rewrite the underlined sentences using the past simple passive.**

Who built Stonehenge and why ¹someone built it continues to be a great mystery. It is one of the most famous prehistoric monuments in the UK. ²Someone started the building of Stonehenge about 5,000 years ago. Some people believe that ³someone used Stonehenge in a celebration of the sun. ⁴Someone designed it in exact mathematical detail, as the stone circle perfectly matches the direction of the midsummer sunrise and the midwinter sunset. There are two types of stone at Stonehenge. The larger stones are called 'sarsens'. The tallest sarsen stands nine metres high and weighs 25 tons – ⁵someone carried the stones 32 kilometres to Stonehenge! The smaller 'bluestones' weigh much less, but ⁶someone brought these stones from Wales, a distance of 225 kilometres. Nobody knows how ⁷someone transported such heavy stones so far in those days.

1 it was built
2 _____
3 _____
4 _____
5 _____
6 _____
7 _____

WRITING
A review

1 ⭐ Look at the photo and read the review. Is everything about the smartwatch positive?

_____

A If you're serious about your fitness training, you'll find this smartwatch very helpful. It counts the calories used in every activity you do. It also gives information on goals, such as distance and speed, and tells you your heart rate. You can connect it to your favourite fitness apps so that your performance can help improve your training.

B This smartwatch is light and comfortable. The strap looks like silk, though it's actually made from soft rubber. It looks cool and modern, and it feels like silk on your skin, too, so you won't know you're wearing it! It's also waterproof, so you can walk straight into the shower after your workout. The battery life is very good: it lasts up to 20 hours and it recharges very quickly.

C What I like about this smartwatch is that it's sporty and strong, but it's also really comfortable so you can wear it all day. However, I should point out that it's not cheap. Overall, I think it's a really cool invention and I'm really happy I bought this model!

2 ⭐⭐ Read the review again. In which paragraph (A–C) can you find …
1 a description of what the invention does [A]
2 what the reviewer likes the most [ ]
3 a physical description [ ]
4 the reviewer's general opinion [ ]
5 a disadvantage [ ]
6 who the invention is for [ ]

3 ⭐⭐ Put the words in the correct order to make the *Useful language* phrases.
1 made from / soft rubber / is / The strap
   The strap is made from soft rubber.
2 it's a / really cool invention / Overall, / I think
   _____
3 it's sporty and strong / about this smartwatch / is that / What I like
   _____
4 it's not cheap / mention that / I should / However,
   _____
5 The strap / looks / silk / like
   _____

Write your own review of an amazing digital device or gadget.

PLAN

4 ⭐⭐ Think of an amazing digital device or gadget. Write notes:

Who the device or gadget is for _____

What it does _____

What it looks like _____

The advantages _____

One disadvantage _____

Your opinion _____

5 Decide what information to include. Use the information in Exercise 2 to help you.

WRITE

6 ⭐⭐⭐ Write your review. Remember to include the parts of the review from Exercise 2, the passive and phrases from the *Useful language* box (see Student's Book, p77).

CHECK

7 Do you …
- describe the device/gadget and who it's for?
- say what the advantages/disadvantages are?
- give your general opinion?

6 REVIEW

VOCABULARY

1 Match the beginnings of the sentences (1–8) with the ends (a–h).

1. If the fruit has stones in it,
2. You should reduce the
3. Don't dip your fingers into
4. Palm oil boils
5. Add the sugar to the water
6. We waited for the liquid to freeze
7. Carefully pour the liquid
8. Pull the paper off the

a. temperature when the sauce gets too hot.
b. at about 300 °C.
c. solid before we ate the lollies.
d. and stir both of them together.
e. into the moulds.
f. remove them before you cook it.
g. ice lollies before the children eat them.
h. very hot water – it's dangerous!

2 <u>Underline</u> and correct one mistake with materials and containers in each sentence.

1. The clothes and shoes were packed in cardboard jars. _____
2. It's better to use glass boxes for jam, so you can recycle them. _____
3. We gave our mum a pretty silk tube for her birthday. _____
4. We don't know what is in this tin bag because there's no label. _____
5. Our teacher always carries our homework and exam papers in a leather can. _____
6. Hospitals have a lot of rubber cases for medical use. _____

LANGUAGE IN ACTION

3 Complete the conversation with the present simple passive form of the verbs in brackets.

BEN Do you know how much coffee ^{1}_____ (make) every year?

HARI I'm sure it's a lot. I know that loads of coffee ^{2}_____ (use) in my house!

BEN Well, they estimate that over two billion cups of coffee ^{3}_____ (drink) worldwide every day.

HARI Wow! That is amazing! And where ^{4}_____ all that coffee _____ (grow)? South America?

BEN Yes, well, most of the coffee which ^{5}_____ (buy) in the UK ^{6}_____ (produce) in Brazil.

HARI I guess the climate is just right there.

BEN Yes, it's perfect because coffee ^{7}_____ (plant) in the wet season, but sunshine ^{8}_____ (need) later in the process. Coffee beans ^{9}_____ (dry) in the sun and ^{10}_____ (test) by experts.

HARI Hmm, how about a cup right now?

BEN Good idea!

4 **Put the words in the correct order to make past simple passive questions. Use the past participle form of the verb. Then write answers using the words in brackets.**

1 was / When / the / build / Taj Mahal / ? (around 1640)

2 open / was / this / When / secondary school / ? (in 2010)

3 were / Where / these / make / computers / ? (in Japan)

4 cave paintings / were / those / Where / old / find / ? (in France)

5 was / Where / tea / grow / first / ? (in China)

6 write / was / When / Macbeth / ? (in 1606)

CUMULATIVE LANGUAGE

5 **Complete the text with the missing words. Circle the correct options.**

I ¹_____ an interesting article about important inventions the other day. ²_____ that plastic shopping bags ³_____ in the 1960s by a Swedish engineer? Before plastic was invented, shoppers ⁴_____ paper bags. These were much better for the environment. Nowadays, governments ⁵_____ to find ways to reduce the use of plastic bags. Ideas include 'Bags for Life'. These bags ⁶_____ of cotton and are very strong, so shoppers can use them again and again. Supermarkets have also ⁷_____ charging customers for their plastic bags. The article also said that scientists believe they ⁸_____ a special bacteria that ⁹_____ eat plastic. The bacteria was discovered in a Japanese recycling centre in 2016. While the scientists ¹⁰_____ the bacteria, they accidentally made it even better at eating plastic! At the moment, the bacteria can only eat the plastic in drinks bottles, but in the future, it ¹¹_____ be able to eat all types of plastic! If scientists ¹²_____ a super bacteria to eat all plastic, plastic bags would become a thing of the past!

1 a read   b have read   c did read
2 a Were you knowing   b Did you knew   c Did you know
3 a was invented   b were invented   c invented
4 a used to use   b use to use   c use to using
5 a try   b tried   c are trying
6 a are made   b is made   c made
7 a begin   b begun   c began
8 a invented   b are invented   c have invented
9 a can   b can to   c can will
10 a investigated   b have investigated   c were investigating
11 a might   b can   c may not
12 a would create   b could create   c might create

UNIT 6 | THINK OUTSIDE THE BOX 55

7 A WORLD OF CELEBRATION

VOCABULARY
Festivals

1 ★ Look at the photos and (circle) the correct options.

2 ★★ Complete the article with the correct form of the words from Exercise 1.

1 a (costume) / decoration

2 an atmosphere / a stall

3 a funfair / parade

4 a parade / float

5 a lantern / firework

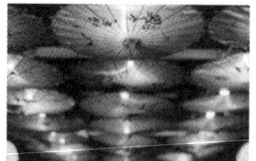
6 a decoration / float

7 a programme / funfair

8 a parade / programme

9 a firework / lantern

One of the biggest festivals in Japan is the Gion Festival in Narita, a small town near Tokyo. It's a celebration of the summer. There are colourful ¹ *decorations* all over the town and people dress up in traditional Japanese ² _____. Visitors can enjoy food and drink at the many ³ _____ in Narita's narrow streets. The best part of the festival is when decorated ⁴ _____ with people on them are pulled through the streets to Narita's main temple. The streets of Narita are beautiful at night when they are lit up by ⁵ _____ on the sides of the buildings.

New Year's Eve is always special in Sydney, Australia. You can see a beautiful display of ⁶ _____ in the night sky, with thousands exploding over the Sydney Opera House. There are lots of things to do during the day, too. Children can enjoy fantastic rides at the ⁷ _____, like a 40–metre big wheel or a super-fast train. In the evening, people love the ⁸ _____ of boats, travelling up and down the harbour with special lights on them!

3 ★★ (Circle) the correct options.
1 There was already (a crowd) / an atmosphere of 50,000 people at ten o'clock!
2 The biggest carnival / ceremony in the world is in Rio, Brazil.
3 Great music and lots of people usually make a good programme / atmosphere.
4 A funfair / ceremony is usually a formal event with a long history.

4 ★★ Underline the stressed syllable in each word.

Two syllables	Three syllables	Four syllables
<u>cos</u>tume	atmosphere	ceremony
firework	carnival	decoration
funfair		
parade		

Explore it!

Guess the correct answer.
The famous Japanese _____ ceremony began around 700 years ago.

a tea   b coffee   c milk

Find an interesting fact about an ancient ceremony. Then send the question in an email to a classmate or ask them in the next class.

56 A WORLD OF CELEBRATION | UNIT 7

READING
A folk tale

1 ⭐ **Look at the pictures. What do you think the folk tale is about? Read the story and (circle) the correct answer.**

   a A prince who lost his son.
   b A very brave dog.
   c A brave prince who killed a wolf.

2 ⭐⭐ **Match the words in bold in the folk tale with the meanings.**

   1 very shocked _horrified_
   2 a long piece of metal used for fighting _____
   3 chasing and trying to catch and kill an animal _____
   4 a place in the ground where dead bodies are _____
   5 strong and not changing in your friendship with someone _____
   6 put something into a hole in the ground and covered it _____

3 ⭐⭐ **Read the folk tale again. (Circle) the correct answers.**

   1 Why did the prince have dogs?
      a Because he was lonely.
      b To look after his castle.
      c To look for other animals.
   2 What did the prince think when he saw blood on his dog?
      a His son was hurt.
      b Something was missing.
      c The dog was hurt.
   3 What did the dog do?
      a Killed the prince's son.
      b Killed a dangerous animal.
      c Hid behind a bed.
   4 What happened at the end?
      a Everyone forgot about the dog.
      b The village was given the dog's name.
      c The prince found another dog.

The wolf and a baby boy

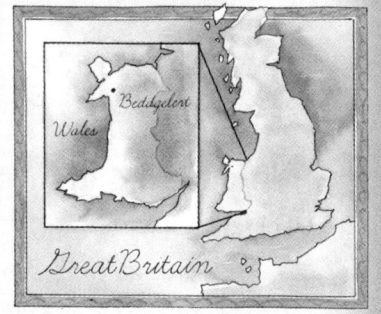

In the north of Wales, there is a small village called Beddgelert. According to an old story, many hundreds of years ago, a prince lived in the area. It was a place of forests and dangerous wild animals. The prince loved **hunting**, so he had lots of dogs. They spent a lot of time chasing animals through the forests for sport. His favourite dog was called Gelert – a **faithful** dog who the prince loved.

One day, the prince decided to go hunting and called for Gelert. To the prince's surprise, the dog came with blood around its mouth. The prince was **horrified**. Where had the blood come from? He had a terrible thought. He ran to his son's bedroom and saw an awful sight. His baby was missing and the floor was covered in blood. The prince realised what the dog had done. With anger, he took a **sword** and killed Gelert. Seconds later, the prince heard a cry from behind the bed. There was his son, completely safe. And next to his son was a wolf – killed by Gelert, just a few minutes earlier. The prince felt very sad. He carried his favourite dog outside and **buried** it under some stones.

Beddgelert means 'Gelert's grave' in the Welsh language, and you can see stones marking the **grave** in the village. However, the story might not be true. Some people say that a hotel owner placed the stones there 200 years ago and, perhaps, invented the story to bring in more tourists. And it worked! Now there are many events in the town, from music festivals to firework displays on New Year's Eve. In the summer, people in the town grow lots of flowers as decorations and Beddgelert has won competitions for being the most beautiful town in the country!

4 ⭐⭐⭐ **Think of a folk tale from your country. Write a paragraph about it in your notebook.**

LANGUAGE IN ACTION
Past perfect

1 ★ Match sentences 1–6 with a–f.
1. I felt very tired. [f]
2. I couldn't go to the concert. [ ]
3. I already knew the story of the film. [ ]
4. I said sorry for being late. [ ]
5. I got lost when I went to London. [ ]
6. I didn't know what time the concert started. [ ]

a I hadn't looked at the programme.
b I hadn't bought any tickets.
c I had read the book.
d I hadn't finished my work on time.
e I hadn't been there before.
f I hadn't slept enough.

2 ★★ Read the sentences. Circle the action that happened first, *A* or *B*.
1. She went to see the fireworks because her friends had invited her.
   A She went to see the fireworks.
   (B) Her friends invited her.
2. When I saw the programme, I knew I'd seen the show before.
   A I saw the programme.
   B I saw the show.
3. They'd arranged to meet at the food stall, but Tom couldn't find Katy.
   A They arranged to meet.
   B Tom couldn't find Katy.
4. After he'd phoned his mum, he ordered a pizza.
   A He ordered a pizza.
   B He phoned his mum.
5. Megan felt a bit upset after she'd said goodbye to them.
   A Megan said goodbye to them.
   B She felt a bit upset.

3 ★★ Complete the sentences with the past perfect form of the verbs in brackets.
1. I __hadn't bought__ (not buy) a costume, so I didn't have anything special to wear to the carnival.
2. Talia _____ (not hear) of the festival before she went there.
3. He got to the concert 20 minutes after it _____ (start).
4. They went to London last year and they were also there 30 years ago. It _____ (change) a lot.
5. We didn't want to see the new *Bond* film because we _____ (not see) the previous one yet.
6. When I got home, I realised that I _____ (leave) my phone at school.

4 ★★ Circle the correct options.

PAULA ¹*Did you go* / *Had you been* anywhere interesting during the holidays?
MARCO Well, I ²*visited* / *had visited* my grandparents in northern Italy in September. They took me to a town called Marostica. I ³*didn't go* / *hadn't been* there before.
PAULA Was it nice?
MARCO Yes, they have a chess festival there.
PAULA Chess festival? That doesn't sound very interesting!
MARCO But it was! My grandparents ⁴*told* / *had told* me a lot about it before I ⁵*went* / *had been* and I'd thought the same as you. But there was a giant chess set in the middle of the town! And people were dressed in costumes as chess pieces and they ⁶*moved* / *had moved* around the board.
PAULA Right, OK. And do they do that every year?
MARCO Every two years. It's to celebrate a famous chess match that two princes ⁷*played* / *had played* about 600 years ago. They ⁸*fell* / *had fallen* in love with the same woman, but instead of fighting, they decided to play chess!

VOCABULARY AND LISTENING
Music festivals and live music

1 ⭐ **Complete the lists with the words in the box. One word can go in more than one list.**

> ~~band member~~ campsite encore
> gig headliner stage support act
> tent track venue

1 where you can see a band: _____
2 where you can stay the night: _____
3 a singer or musician in a group: band member

2 ⭐⭐ **Complete the text with the correct form of the words from Exercise 1.**

> The ¹ venue for Glastonbury Festival is a farm in England. Thousands of music fans go there to see their favourite bands. ² _____ at Glastonbury have included some of the biggest names in music, like Radiohead and Katy Perry. There are also lots of interesting, less famous ³ _____ to see. These bands play on smaller ⁴ _____ in front of smaller crowds. Visitors to the festival usually stay on a big ⁵ _____ with thousands of ⁶ _____ . There's always a great atmosphere at Glastonbury and the bands always leave the fans shouting for an ⁷ _____ !

A conversation

3 🎧 7.01 ⭐ **Listen to the conversation. What is unusual about the Secret Solstice Festival?**

_____

4 🎧 7.01 ⭐⭐ **Listen again. Are the sentences T (true) or F (false)?**

1 Brandon hasn't been to the Secret Solstice Festival. __T__
2 The weather isn't very cold at the festival. _____
3 Famous bands don't play at the festival. _____
4 One of the venues is in a dangerous place. _____
5 Brandon's brother didn't have tickets for the volcano gig. _____

5 ⭐⭐ **Look at Exercise 6. What type of information (object, number or place) is missing in 1–7? (See the *Learn to learn* tip in the Student's Book, p86).**

_____

6 🎧 7.01 ⭐⭐⭐ **Complete the summary about the Secret Solstice festival. Then listen again and check.**

> The Secret Solstice is a festival. It takes place each year in ¹ Iceland during the summer solstice. Brandon says the festival feels like a ² _____ -hour day. When Brandon's brother went, there were about ³ _____ bands. One venue at the festival was inside a volcano. You needed to fly in a ⁴ _____ to get there and then go down ⁵ _____ metres to reach the venue. Only ⁶ _____ people could see the gig and the tickets cost about ⁷ _____ pounds each.

UNIT 7 | A WORLD OF CELEBRATION 59

LANGUAGE IN ACTION
Reported statements

1 ⭐ **How do the tenses and verbs change in reported speech? Complete the table.**

Direct speech	Reported speech
present simple	[1] past simple
past simple	[2]
present perfect	[3]
present continuous	[4]
will	[5]
can	[6]

2 ⭐ **Complete the sentences with *said* or *told*.**

1 My sister ___said___ she went to a really interesting music festival last year.
2 George _____ me that he had some new tracks for me to listen to.
3 I _____ everyone that I had a spare ticket for the concert.
4 Sally _____ that she couldn't go to the campsite because she didn't have a tent.
5 Laura _____ us to meet her in front of the stage.
6 I _____ I didn't know who the support act was.

3 ⭐⭐ **Rewrite the reported speech as direct speech.**

1 Ashraf said that he was in a café.
   'I'm in a café.'
2 He told me that he was having lunch.
   '_____'
3 He said he wanted to meet me.
   '_____'
4 He said that he had been in the café for an hour.
   '_____'
5 He told me he would leave in about 30 minutes.
   '_____'
6 He told me to come quickly.
   '_____'

4 ⭐⭐ **Read the conversation. Then complete the reported speech below.**

ME	Hi, Ashraf!
ASHRAF	Hi! I'm really happy to see you! I have some exciting news. I'm thinking of going to a festival in the summer. I want you to come with me.
ME	Hmm, I'm not sure. Where is it? How much is it?
ASHRAF	It's not far away. It's in the countryside. The tickets are about £30. I've been there before. I had a great time.
ME	OK, but where would we stay?
ASHRAF	Well, there's a campsite. We can stay in a tent. It won't be expensive.
ME	OK, I'll think about it.
ASHRAF	Great!

I went to the café to meet Ashraf. He said that he [1] ___was___ happy to see me and that he [2] _____ some exciting news. He told me that he [3] _____ of going to a festival in the summer, and then he told me that he [4] _____ me to go with him. I said that I [5] _____ sure, and I asked where the festival was and how much it was. Ashraf said that it [6] _____ far away, in the countryside, and the tickets [7] _____ about £30. He said that he [8] _____ there before and that he [9] _____ a great time. He also said that we [10] _____ in a tent, so it [11] _____ very expensive. I said that I [12] _____ about it.

5 ⭐⭐⭐ **Think of a conversation you had with someone recently. What did you talk about? Write at least five sentences using reported speech.**

I was talking to Mum yesterday. She told me …
_____
_____
_____
_____

A WORLD OF CELEBRATION | UNIT 7

WRITING
An email to a friend

1 ⭐ Read the email quickly. (Circle) the photo that matches it.

From: Karen   **To:** Matt

¹Hello Matt,

²I just got your message, thanks. ³It was nice of you to write!

You said you wanted to know all about the festival. I'd never been to anything like it before, but it was great! I only spent a day there, but I saw so many amazing things. There were lots of people dressed as characters from film and TV. I'm attaching a photo of some people I met. That's Spiderman on the left! He told me to say hello to you! I think I was the only one not wearing a costume! I felt strange walking around in normal clothes!

In the afternoon, there was an event with some really famous actors from *Star Wars*. There were probably around 500 people in the audience, asking questions. Unfortunately, I didn't get the chance to ask anything. But one of the guests said that she had just filmed something really exciting for the next film. Then she told us! I can't say anything – it's a spoiler!

OK, ⁴I must go now. ⁵I hope to hear from you soon.

⁶I'll be in touch later,

Karen

2 ⭐⭐ Put a–e in the order they appear in the email (1–5).
a ☐ request for a reply
b ☐ goodbye
c ☐ description of the festival
d [1] greeting
e ☐ thanks for writing

3 ⭐⭐ Match the underlined phrases in the email (1–6) with the *Useful language* phrases (a–f).
a Write back soon. [5]
b Anyway, that's all from me. ☐
c Bye for now. ☐
d Hi Matt, ☐
e It was great to hear from you. ☐
f Thanks for your email. ☐

Write your own email about a festival.

PLAN

4 ⭐⭐ Think of a festival you have been to. Write notes.

What kind of festival was it? _____

What did people wear? _____

What did people do? _____

What did you see and do? _____

How did you feel? _____

5 Decide what information to include. Use the structure in Exercise 2 to help you.

WRITE

6 Write your email. Remember to include the past perfect, reported speech and phrases from the *Useful language* box (see Student's Book, p89).

CHECK

7 Do you …
• have a greeting and a goodbye?
• describe the ceremony?
• request a reply?

7 REVIEW

VOCABULARY

1 **Match the definitions with the words in the box.**

> costume   decoration
> firework   float   funfair
> lantern   parade
> programme   stall

1 something you use to make things look more interesting or beautiful

2 a plan of all the activities and events at a festival

3 a big table on the street where people can buy things

4 a big decorated lorry that moves through the streets at festivals

5 a light that people can hold or hang up in public places

6 the clothes you wear for a special activity

7 something that makes beautiful lights and noises in the night sky

8 a large number of people walking together, usually to celebrate something

9 a place with games and machines you can ride on

2 **Complete the sentences with words for music and live festivals.**

1 There were three b_____ m_____ in Clean Bandit: Grace Chatto, and Jack and Luke Patterson.

2 At the end of the concert, the audience shouted for more and the band came back for an e_____ .

3 It was a terrible v_____ for a concert. I couldn't see the stage because it was really far away.

4 I don't think this year's festival will be very good. The h_____ are a band from the 1990s that no one has heard of.

5 We went to a small g_____ last night – it was one of the best live events I've been to.

6 Did you know that there is a bonus t_____ at the end of the album? Most people don't know about it.

7 Sometimes, the s_____ a_____ is better than the main performer.

8 The festival has a big c_____ with space for nearly 500 tents.

LANGUAGE IN ACTION

3 **Complete the sentences with the past perfect form of the verbs in the box.**

> be   book   decorate   hear   not see   sell

1 I didn't go to the festival because I _____ that it was going to rain.

2 I'm glad that we _____ the tickets early, because they became really expensive later.

3 By the time the headliners appeared, the support acts _____ on stage for an hour.

4 My sister loved the concert. She _____ anything like it before.

5 When you checked the tickets online, _____ they _____ them all?

6 People _____ the street with lanterns and it looked beautiful.

62 A WORLD OF CELEBRATION | UNIT 7

4 What did Mike say? Change the direct speech into reported speech.

1 'I want to go home.'
Mike said that _____

2 'I don't feel well.'
Mike said that _____

3 'I've taken some medicine.'
Mike said that _____

4 'I'll take a taxi home'
Mike said that _____

5 'I can't find a taxi number!'
Mike said that _____

6 'I'll ask my mum to collect me.'
Mike said that _____

CUMULATIVE LANGUAGE

5 Complete the text with the missing words. Circle the correct options.

I live in a small town. It's nice, but nothing interesting ever ¹_____. So I was really surprised when my dad ²_____ me that there would be a big celebration. He said that the bridge in the town ³_____ 200 years old this summer and there would be a huge party. At first, I said that I wasn't interested. I ⁴_____ over that bridge thousands of times going to school and I ⁵_____ see it in my summer holidays. But then my dad said, 'If you ⁶_____ to the festival, you'll have a great time'. So I went. And it really was great! Everyone was dressed up in costumes and they had a parade through the town centre. The whole town ⁷_____ like a big history lesson! And in the evening, there ⁸_____ a big fireworks display. Earlier that day, I ⁹_____ that the bridge was really important in history. It ¹⁰_____ by a famous architect. I ¹¹_____ it was just a boring bridge! It was a great day, but I still don't think there are ¹²_____ in my town!

	a	b	c
1	happens	had happened	is happening
2	said	asked	told
3	is being	should be	would be
4	was	had	have been
5	not want	didn't want to	didn't wanted
6	came	will come	come
7	looks	looking	looked
8	was	were	had been
9	was learning	have learned	had learned
10	is built	built	was built
11	was thinking	used to think	don't think
12	festivals enough	too festivals	enough festivals

8 BACK TO SCHOOL

VOCABULARY
School

1 ⭐ (Circle) the correct verbs to complete the phrases about school.

1 (cheat) / pay in a test
2 tell / fail an exam
3 get / pay detention
4 revise / get good grades
5 hand / pass in homework on time
6 cheat / pass an exam
7 pay / get attention to the teacher
8 revise / take for a test
9 take / pay an exam
10 say / tell somebody off
11 write / revise an essay

2 ⭐ Look at phrases 1–8 in Exercise 1. Write them in the correct column.

Positive things	Negative things
	cheat in a test

3 ⭐⭐ Complete the sentences with the correct form of phrases from Exercise 1.

1 I _took an exam_ last week but I'm not sure how well I did.
2 If you _____ for bad behaviour, you won't be able to go to rugby practice after school!
3 He doesn't always _____ for his school work – last week he got a D for an essay.
4 Paula was very pleased when she _____ all her _____ – she got As in the history and science!
5 I can't go out tonight. I need to _____ on capital cities and I haven't learned them all yet.
6 I _____ on ancient history – I got an F! I need to take it again.
7 Why did the teacher _____ you _____? What did you do to make him angry?
8 Please try to _____ on time, Sam! That's the second time you've given it to me late this week!
9 Someone _____ in Miss Clarke's class. They used their phone to look for the answers!
10 Unless you _____ and listen to everything he says, you won't know how to do the project.

4 ⭐⭐⭐ Complete the sentences so they are true for you.

1 If I saw someone cheating in a test, I would
_____.

2 It's important for me to get good grades because
_____.

3 The last time I failed an exam was
_____.

4 One important exam I will take this year is
_____.

5 I usually revise for tests
_____.

Explore it!

Guess the correct answer.

The highest school in the world is called Phumachangtang in the Himalayas. The school is more than *4,000 / 5,000 / 6,000* metres above sea level.

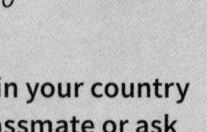

Find an interesting fact about education in your country and send the question in an email to a classmate or ask them in the next class.

READING
A report

1 ⭐ What do you think is happening in the photo? Read the report and check your ideas.

SCHOOL'S OUT

Almost 50,000 people were homeschooled in the UK last year. **Reasons** for homeschooling can include a child's special needs, **bullying** or **a lack of** good school options in the area. We spoke to one 'homeschooler', Andrew James, from Cumbria in the UK, about his experiences of homeschooling.

'I started homeschooling three years ago – I'm 14 now. When I left junior school, I went straight to homeschooling, so I've never been to secondary school. My mum was also homeschooled, so she was **keen** for us to have a similar education to hers. My parents believe that education is not just about getting good grades or taking exams – they think a **balanced** education, including practical skills, is also important.

My younger brother and I study at home with our parents for seven hours a day. Both our parents used to be teachers – so that helps! But having school at home doesn't mean there aren't any rules. We're not allowed to stay in bed all day, obviously, but we can also choose what we learn. Of course, we study normal subjects, but we also frequently go to libraries, museums, exhibitions, concerts and sporting events as part of our education.

We can also do other things that maybe you can't do at an ordinary school. For example, each year my brother and I are allowed to plan a big trip to a place connected to something we are studying. My brother studies geology, so we went to Mount Vesuvius in Italy to learn about volcanoes.

Next year, I want to go to Amsterdam to visit the house of Anne Frank because I'm learning about her famous **diary** in my history lessons.

It's not all holidays and day trips – we work really hard and study a lot! But I really love my home education. I wouldn't change it for anything!'

2 ⭐⭐ Match the words in bold in the report with the meanings.
  1 having equal amounts of something   _balanced_
  2 a book with someone's thoughts and feelings _____
  3 the causes of an event or situation _____
  4 very interested in _____
  5 not enough of something _____
  6 when someone hurts or frightens someone else _____

3 ⭐⭐ Read the report again. Are the sentences T (true) or F (false)? Correct the false sentences.
  1 Andrew has never attended an ordinary school.
     F. He went to an ordinary junior school.
  2 Andrew started homeschooling because he didn't like his school.
     _____
  3 His parents taught at schools before they homeschooled Andrew.
     _____
  4 Andrew and his brother do some studying outside their home.
     _____
  5 Their trips to other places are part of their education.
     _____
  6 Andrew would like to go back to ordinary school in the future.
     _____

4 ⭐⭐⭐ Think of two possible disadvantages of homeschooling.

LANGUAGE IN ACTION
can/can't

1 ⭐ **What do the sentences express? Write *permission*, *prohibition* or *ability*.**

1. Marcus can't leave yet because he's got detention. _____
2. You had a very good grade for your essay. Can I read it? _____
3. Sonia can play two instruments and she's a great singer, too. _____

2 ⭐ **Circle the correct options.**

1. In my school, we **can** / *can't* learn Latin if we want.
2. My sister *can* / *can't* speak Italian, but she speaks German well.
3. Mrs Evans says I *can* / *can't* leave until I've finished this exercise.
4. *Can* / *Can't* I borrow your dictionary, please?
5. We *can* / *can't* understand you when you speak clearly.
6. You *can* / *can't* stay in bed all day. It's bad for you.

be allowed to

3 ⭐⭐ **Put the words in the correct order to make sentences. Then tick (✓) the sentences that are true for your school.**

1. school / at / wear / allowed / Students / aren't / jewellery / to
   Students aren't allowed to wear jewellery at school. ☐
2. lunchtime / allowed / phones / We / at / use / to / are / our
   _____ ☐
3. break time / football / play / Students / at / are / allowed / to
   _____ ☐
4. shout / allowed / aren't / the / You / teachers / to / at
   _____ ☐

4 ⭐⭐ **Write questions and short answers with the correct form of *be allowed to*.**

1. you / cycle to school? (yes)
   Are you allowed to cycle to school?   Yes, I am.
2. your teachers / give detention? (yes)
   _____
3. boys / wear any clothes they like? (no)
   _____
4. students / talk in exams? (no)
   _____
5. your best friend / sit next to you? (yes)
   _____
6. your parents / help with homework? (no)
   _____

5 ⭐⭐ **Complete the conversation with the missing words. Circle the correct options.**

I think it's hard to be the youngest in the family. My big sister ¹_____ to go to bed when she wants, but I ²_____. On Fridays and Saturdays I ³_____ stay up later, but not as late as my sister. And my big brothers ⁴_____ watch late shows on TV! But they ⁵_____ to leave the house without helping our parents. They ⁶_____ go to college by car, but I ⁷_____ drive yet so I cycle to school. All the people in my family ⁸_____ tell me off because I'm the youngest – it's so unfair!

1. **a** is allowed   b are allowed   c can
2. a can   b 'm not   c isn't
3. a can't   b can   c 'm not allowed to
4. a can to   b is allowed to   c are allowed to
5. a aren't allowed   b can't   c not allowed
6. a can   b can't   c aren't allowed to
7. a 'm allowed to   b can   c can't
8. a are allowed to   b is allowed to   c aren't allowed to

LISTENING AND VOCABULARY
A phone call

1 ⭐ You will hear an exchange student in the Netherlands talking about what she likes about the country. Write two questions you'd like to ask.

_____
_____

🎧 **2** ⭐⭐ Listen to the phone call. Does it answer any of your questions from Exercise 1?
8.01

_____

🎧 **3** ⭐⭐ Listen again and answer the questions.
8.01
1 What is the subject of the phone call?
   Studying and living in another country.
2 How long will Julia be in the Netherlands?
   _____
3 What's her favourite thing about life in the Netherlands?
   _____
4 Why are Dutch drivers usually polite, according to Julia?
   _____
5 How did Julia travel to school this morning?
   _____
6 Which country does Julia compare with the Netherlands?
   _____

Attitude and behaviour

4 ⭐ Complete the words with the correct vowels (*a, e, i, o, u*).

1 r u d e
2 c _ r _ f _ l
3 ch _ ld _ sh
4 p _ l _ t _
5 m _ t _ r _
6 c _ r _ l _ ss
7 _ rg _ n _ s _ d
8 n _ _ ghty
9 d _ s _ rg _ n _ s _ d
10 w _ ll-b _ h _ v _ d

5 ⭐⭐ Complete the sentences with the words from Exercise 4.
1 Rohan is a very _well-behaved_ student: the teachers never need to tell him off.
2 Patricia is a very _____ child. She never says please!
3 Our teacher likes us to be _____ and keep our desks clean and tidy.
4 Please be _____ when you cycle in the rain.
5 Don't be _____ – you should check your homework for mistakes before you hand it in.
6 Our parents teach us to be _____ and thank visitors for coming to the house.
7 Bella's pens and pencils are all over the floor. She's so _____ with her things!
8 My little cousin is very _____! My aunt's always telling him off, but he never listens.
9 Molly is nearly 16, but sometimes she is very _____ – like a little girl.
10 Paul is younger than his sister Molly, but he's much more _____ and sensible.

6 ⭐⭐ Match sentences 1–5 with a–e.
1 Jorge is so careless.   [c]
2 He's usually very mature.   [ ]
3 Ben's a naughty boy at home.   [ ]
4 Try to be more polite.   [ ]
5 Eymen isn't disorganised.   [ ]

a He hardly ever does anything childish.
b It's so rude not to say thank you.
c He should try to be more careful.
d His schoolwork is always tidy and organised.
e But he's well-behaved at school.

UNIT 8 | BACK TO SCHOOL 67

LANGUAGE IN ACTION
have to, must and need to

1 ★ Circle the correct options.
1. You *need to / don't have to / mustn't* revise for exams.
2. He *must / doesn't need to / doesn't have to* be better-behaved in class – he's quite naughty!
3. Students *don't have to / don't need to / mustn't* wear make-up: it's not allowed.
4. We *don't need to / have to / mustn't* ask if we don't understand the questions.
5. You *don't have to / must / have to* finish the essay right now. It's for next week.

2 ★★ Put the words in the correct order to make the Exam FAQs.

Exam FAQs
1. need / we / to / an optional question / answer / Do / ?
   Do we need to answer an optional question?
2. have / we / Do / to / a pen / use / ?
   _____
3. do / What / first / need / to / we / do / ?
   _____
4. if / we / What / have / do / to / do / not sure / we're / ?
   _____
5. do / need / What / to / we / do / before / finish / we / ?
   _____
6. have / we / to / Do / the exam room / stay / in / ?
   _____

4 ★★ Are the sentences about the school notices *T* (true) or *F* (false)? Correct the false sentences with (*don't*) *have to* or *must* (*n't*). Sometimes there is more than one possible answer.

1. School nurse available Monday, Wednesday, Friday only. Please make an appointment.
2. Mobile phone calls allowed in canteen
3. SILENCE OUTSIDE THE LIBRARY ON MONDAY MORNING: EXAMS!
4. Seniors' leaving party: June 14th Funny costumes optional!

1. You don't have to make an appointment to see the nurse.
   F. You have to / must make an appointment to see the nurse.
2. Students don't have to switch off their phones in the canteen.
   _____
3. You mustn't make noise outside the library on Monday morning.
   _____
4. Students must wear a funny costume to the leaving party.
   _____

3 ★★ Complete the sentences with the phrases in the box. Then match the answers (a–f) with the FAQs (1–6) in Exercise 2.

| don't have to stay   don't need to answer   have to use   have to write   ~~need to check~~   need to read |

a. You *need to check* all your answers before you finish.
b. You _____ in the room, but please leave quietly.
c. You _____ all the questions carefully before you answer.
d. If a question is optional, you _____ it.
e. Yes, you _____ a black pen.
f. You _____ something, so if you're not sure about an answer, don't leave it – guess!

WRITING
An essay

1 ⭐ Make a list of the advantages and disadvantages of digital technology in school education. Then read the essay. Does it have your ideas?

_____
_____

Should we reduce digital technology in the classroom?

A Most of us find it difficult to imagine schools without laptops or tablets, but some people believe that using electronic devices in class too much can be a bad thing. ¹<u>essay, / In / outline / I / this</u> some of the advantages and disadvantages of technology and give my own opinion.

B ²<u>hand, / the / On / one</u> using digital technology in the classroom can be more exciting than learning from books. Technology can also encourage more students to take part in group work through online activities. It is also believed that using technology can help students to remember what they learn.

C ³<u>other / On / the / hand,</u> technology may cause students to stop paying attention in class. ⁴<u>that / Some / say</u> technology is also bad for social skills, as students might speak to each other less during lessons. ⁵<u>argue / that / Others</u> technology can make cheating easier for students – both in classwork and homework.

D In my opinion, there are more important advantages than disadvantages, but there should be a balance between technology and traditional classroom work. Computers can never take the place of the teacher!

2 ⭐ Match the parts of the essay (1–4) with the correct paragraphs (A–D).
1. a conclusion with the writer's opinion D
2. bad things about digital technology ____
3. an introduction to the topic ____
4. good things about digital technology ____

3 ⭐⭐ Put the underlined words in the essay in the correct order to make the *Useful language* phrases.

1. In this essay, I outline   4. _____
2. _____   5. _____
3. _____

> Write your own essay.
>
> **PLAN**
>
> **4** ⭐⭐ Think of two good things and two bad things about weekend homework. Write notes.
>
> | Good things | _____ |
> | Bad things | _____ |
>
> **5** Look at the essay question. Make notes on your opinion and decide what to include. Use the information in Exercise 2.
>
> Is weekend homework a good or bad thing?
>
> **WRITE**
>
> **6** ⭐⭐⭐ Write your essay. Remember to include four paragraphs, *can/can't, be allowed to, have to, must* and *need to* and the phrases from the *Useful language* box (see Student's Book, p101).
>
> **CHECK**
>
> **7** Do you …
> - have an introduction and conclusion?
> - write about good things and bad things?

UNIT 8 | BACK TO SCHOOL 69

8 REVIEW

VOCABULARY

1 Match the beginnings of the sentences (1–6) with the ends (a–f).

1 The teacher will tell you off if ☐
2 If you revise well for a test, ☐
3 It's always wrong ☐
4 If students don't pay attention, ☐
5 We usually have to write an essay ☐
6 If you work, you won't fail ☐

a when we take an English exam.
b the exam – you'll pass it.
c they won't know what to do.
d you'll get a good grade.
e to cheat in a test.
f you don't hand in homework on time.

2 Circle the correct words.

1 Jonty is very *well-behaved / naughty*: he never gets detention.
2 It's *polite / rude* to talk when your teacher's talking.
3 I'm so *organised / disorganised* that I can never find anything.
4 She's only ten but she's really *mature / childish* for her age.
5 *Careful / Careless* work doesn't usually get good grades.
6 You're so *well-behaved / naughty*. You never do anything I tell you!
7 *Childish / Mature* people behave like someone a lot younger.
8 Be *careless / careful* with Ahmet – he's very sensitive!
9 He's very *rude / polite*: he always says 'please' and 'thank you'.
10 Very *organised / disorganised* people plan everything they do.

LANGUAGE IN ACTION

3 Complete the sentences with *can*, *can't* or the correct form of *be allowed*.

1 In some countries, girls _____ go to school because their parents need their help.
2 Boys in that school _____ to wear long trousers. They all wear shorts.
3 We _____ to have smartphones in the exam room: that's cheating.
4 You _____ use the library after lunch but not in the morning.
5 If you're late for an exam, you _____ to take it – you have to do it another day.
6 Your parents _____ help you because they don't know Latin.

4 Complete the sentences with the words in the box.

> have to wear   have to worry   must be   mustn't run   need to come   need to meet

1 You really _____ quick. The test starts soon.
2 We don't _____ school uniform at the weekend.
3 Sally doesn't _____ . She's revised well for the test.
4 My parents _____ my teacher after school.
5 We _____ in the corridors. It's dangerous.
6 Do I _____ with you or can you go alone?

CUMULATIVE LANGUAGE

5 Complete the text with the missing words. Circle the correct options.

HOME   ABOUT ME   ARCHIVE   FOLLOW

Hello! In this week's blog I ¹_____ at exam preparation. Now, if you usually ²_____ my blog, you'll know that I hate exams. I just ³_____ do them! If I ⁴_____ make exams history, I would do it! Anyway, I ⁵_____ this subject a lot since my last post and I think one important thing is planning: you ⁶_____ start revising well before your exams. You ⁷_____ start months before, but at least a ⁸_____ weeks. You ⁹_____ also study at school as well as at home. Find a quiet place, like the library, so you ¹⁰_____ concentrate. Little and often is the best way to study; an hour a day is great. Also, do exercise between study sessions – this helps you to relax. I ¹¹_____ for a run in my local park. Finally, get a good night's sleep before the exam! In my last exam, I ¹²_____ well the night before and I got a really bad grade. OK, that's all for now. More tips next week!

1 a	look	b 'm looking	c had looked
2 a	read	b will read	c have read
3 a	can	b can't to	c can't
4 a	could	b can	c would
5 a	'm studying	b 've studied	c 'd studied
6 a	must	b don't have to	c must to
7 a	have to	b haven't to	c don't have to
8 a	few	b little	c enough
9 a	shouldn't	b should	c should to
10 a	need to	b have to	c 'll be able to
11 a	'm going often	b go often	c often go
12 a	hadn't slept	b haven't slept	c wasn't sleeping

UNIT 8 | BACK TO SCHOOL 71

9 A HOLIDAY ON THE MOON

VOCABULARY
Travel

1 ⭐⭐ Complete the puzzle. Use the clues.

1. the place someone is travelling to
2. in or to a different country from yours
3. a family place with hotels, pools, restaurants and bars (two words)
4. when you travel somewhere and go back home in a short time
5. a large boat that you can have a holiday on (two words)
6. when you visit a place and look around it, often with a group of people
7. when you travel from one place to another, especially in transport
8. a place to stay on holiday, e.g. a hotel, caravan or youth hostel
9. travelling with a large bag, usually visiting many places
10. visiting famous or interesting places on holiday
11. a reservation you make to have a hotel room, or a seat on a plane.

2 ⭐⭐ What is the hidden word in grey in the puzzle in Exercise 1?

3 ⭐⭐ Complete the text with the correct form of the words from Exercise 1. Sometimes more than one answer is possible.

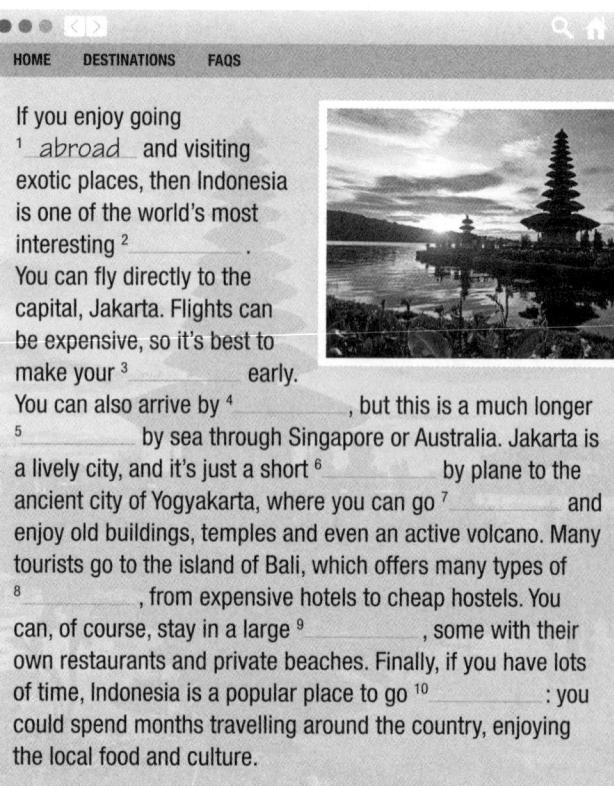

HOME   DESTINATIONS   FAQS

If you enjoy going ¹ _abroad_ and visiting exotic places, then Indonesia is one of the world's most interesting ² _____. You can fly directly to the capital, Jakarta. Flights can be expensive, so it's best to make your ³ _____ early. You can also arrive by ⁴ _____, but this is a much longer ⁵ _____ by sea through Singapore or Australia. Jakarta is a lively city, and it's just a short ⁶ _____ by plane to the ancient city of Yogyakarta, where you can go ⁷ _____ and enjoy old buildings, temples and even an active volcano. Many tourists go to the island of Bali, which offers many types of ⁸ _____, from expensive hotels to cheap hostels. You can, of course, stay in a large ⁹ _____, some with their own restaurants and private beaches. Finally, if you have lots of time, Indonesia is a popular place to go ¹⁰ _____: you could spend months travelling around the country, enjoying the local food and culture.

Explore it!

Guess the correct answer.

A cruise ship creates the same amount of pollution in one day as … cars.

a 5,000   b 20,000   c 1 million

Find an interesting fact about tourism and the environment and send the question in an email to a classmate or ask them in the next class.

READING
A magazine interview

1 ⭐ **Look at the photos of drones. Then read the interview and (circle) the best title.**
   a The dangers of drones
   b Why drones will never solve transport problems
   c How drones will change the way we travel

2 ⭐⭐ **Match the words in bold with the definitions.**
   1 staying away from someone or something _avoiding_
   2 taking things like food or books to someone's house _____
   3 working quickly and in an organised way _____
   4 arrive on the ground after moving down through the air _____
   5 not having a driver _____
   6 big vehicles used to transport things _____

3 ⭐⭐ **Read the interview again. Complete it with the missing questions (1–5).**
   1 Isn't this going to create lots of problems?
   2 Won't this make people lazy?
   3 What other changes will there be?
   4 ~~How will we be travelling in the future?~~
   5 What are the advantages?

4 ⭐⭐ **Read the interview again. Answer the questions.**
   1 How will companies save money with new technology?
   They will use driverless trucks.
   2 Where might we see flying taxis soon?
   _____
   3 What might be the biggest danger for flying taxis?
   _____
   4 What three things make flying taxis better than normal taxis?
   _____
   5 How will drones help people in danger?
   _____

THE SKY'S THE LIMIT!

Computer scientist Jeremy May answers our questions about the future of transport.

A How will we be travelling in the future?
I think **driverless** taxis will become common. Not only that, but companies will soon be using **trucks** which don't have a driver. This will save companies a lot of money. Some companies have developed a kind of flying taxi, too. It works like a helicopter, but it doesn't need a pilot — it's actually a drone. It's possible that some cities, like Dubai, will have lots of flying taxis in the near future.

B _____
Well, some people are worried that driverless taxis aren't safe. Flying taxis have to be even safer, of course. The skies are already full, so one challenge will be **avoiding** objects, like other drones, buildings and birds. But most of us won't need to worry. It's likely that only the very rich will be able to travel by flying taxi — in the beginning anyway.

C _____
Firstly, these taxis will use electricity, so they will be more environmentally friendly. Secondly, they will be able to travel up to 180 kilometres per hour. This, plus the fact that they will be able to take off and **land** anywhere, means that they will be much more **efficient** than normal taxis.

D _____
Companies will soon start **delivering** things by drone. In Dubai, a company tested a service for people who wanted a coffee but didn't want to travel to a café. The people just ordered online and got their coffee in a few minutes!

E _____
It might! But the technology has a more serious use. We will be using drones to send quickly medicines or food to difficult-to-reach places like mountains or islands. This will be very useful in emergencies.

UNIT 9 | A HOLIDAY ON THE MOON 73

LANGUAGE IN ACTION
be going to and present continuous for future

1 ☆ Complete the sentences with the phrases in the box. Then write *A* for the arrangements and *P* for the predictions.

> aren't going to find   is going to make
> 'm going to   're travelling   's leaving

1 Next week, I 'm going to Spain on holiday. A
2 He _____ for the airport in an hour by taxi. ___
3 Technology _____ travel more environmentally friendly. ___
4 We _____ to Bali by plane, not cruise ship. ___
5 They _____ a way to travel which is 100% safe. ___

2 ☆☆ Decide if the sentences are arrangements or predictions. Then complete them with the best form of the verb in brackets.

1 I 'm meeting (meet) my friend at four o'clock on Saturday.
2 She _____ (not enjoy) the journey by cruise ship next week – she hates boats.
3 We _____ (go) camping in Greece in July.
4 They _____ (like) Madagascar next summer. The wildlife there is incredible!
5 Todd and Laura _____ (have) lunch at the airport tomorrow before their flight.

Future continuous

3 ☆☆ Put the words in order to make sentences in the future continuous. Then tick (✓) the sentences you agree with.

1 abroad / in / I / 20 / living / be / years / will
   I will be living abroad in 20 years.
2 will / by 2025 / be / travelling / by flying taxi / Everyone
   _____
3 doing / all / Robots / jobs / in / will / be / ten years
   _____
4 50 years / living / other / won't / We / be / planets / on / in
   _____
5 using / won't / be / 15 years / petrol / We / in / cars / in
   _____

4 ☆☆ Circle the best options. For one answer, both options are possible.

I read the other day that we ¹*are living /(will be living)* on Mars in the next 30 years. Well, you and I ²*aren't going to live / aren't living* on Mars – they ³*are only sending / are only going to send* their top astronauts in the near future! Normal people ⁴*aren't living / won't be living* there for a long time. The famous scientist Professor Stephen Hawking said that we ⁵*are going to need / are needing* to find a new planet in 100 years because we ⁶*are having / are going to have* more problems with climate change and other things in the future. I ⁷*'m giving / 'm going to give* a presentation on space travel next week at school, so I've done some research! Hawking had previously said that in 1,000 years, people ⁸*aren't living / won't be living* on the Earth at all. I'm not sure I agree – a lot of things can happen in 1,000 years!

5 ☆☆☆ Write three predictions in the future continuous. Use the ideas in the box or your own ideas.

> communication   houses   music
> relationships   work

By 2050, people won't be communicating face-to-face anymore.
_____
_____
_____
_____

VOCABULARY AND LISTENING
Travel phrasal verbs

1 ⭐ Complete the phrasal verbs in the sentences. Use the words in the box.

> around   away   back   in   off   out

1 After we've checked __in__ to our hotel, I want to rest and then have some lunch.
2 We didn't go _____ this summer. We stayed at home for our holidays.
3 I always feel nervous when the plane is taking _____.
4 We have to check _____ of the hotel early – at 9 o'clock – but we can leave our bags.
5 Our plane is at 2 pm, so we need to set _____ for the airport at around 11 am.
6 I went to Madrid for a short business trip, but I didn't have time to look _____ the city.
7 It's nice to get _____ on holiday once a year and see a new place.
8 Our train was delayed, so we didn't get _____ until late at night.
9 What time is your plane expected to get _____?

2 ⭐⭐ Complete the email with the correct form of the phrasal verbs from Exercise 1.

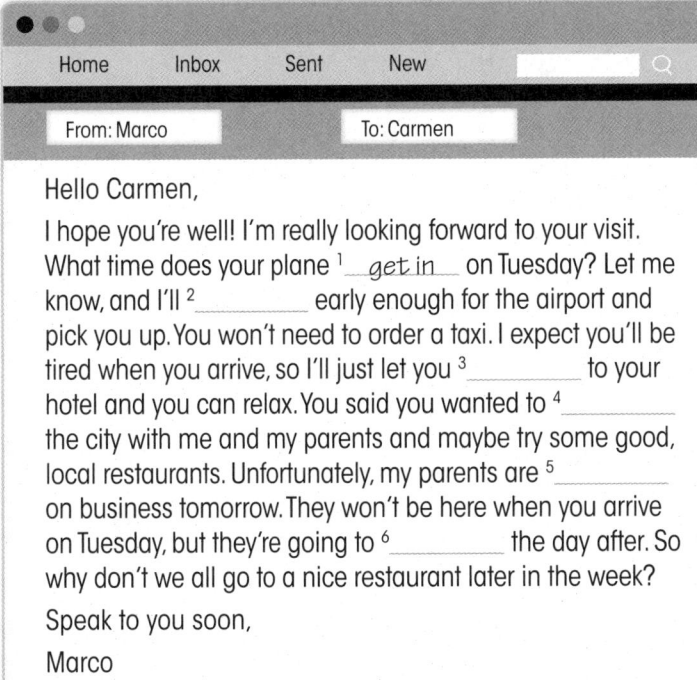

Hello Carmen,

I hope you're well! I'm really looking forward to your visit. What time does your plane ¹ _get in_ on Tuesday? Let me know, and I'll ² _____ early enough for the airport and pick you up. You won't need to order a taxi. I expect you'll be tired when you arrive, so I'll just let you ³ _____ to your hotel and you can relax. You said you wanted to ⁴ _____ the city with me and my parents and maybe try some good, local restaurants. Unfortunately, my parents are ⁵ _____ on business tomorrow. They won't be here when you arrive on Tuesday, but they're going to ⁶ _____ the day after. So why don't we all go to a nice restaurant later in the week?

Speak to you soon,
Marco

Conversations

3 ⭐ You will hear two people planning a holiday. Look at the map and answer the questions.

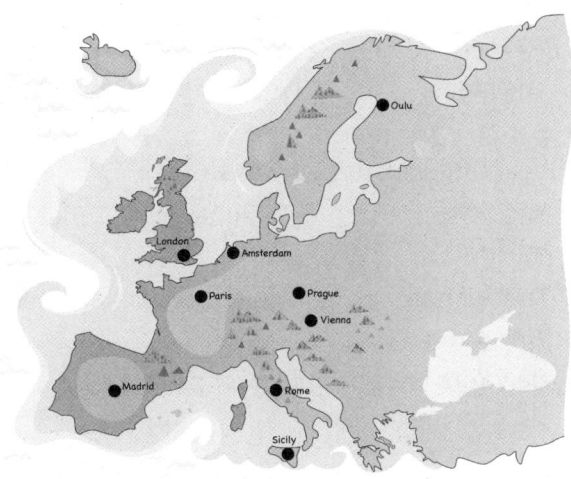

1 Which part of the world are they going to visit?
   _____
2 What's the best way to travel around and see all these places?
   _____
3 How much time do you think you would need?
   _____

4 🎧 9.01 ⭐ Listen to the conversation and check your answers to Exercise 3. Do Emma and Mason have the same ideas as you for questions 2 and 3?
   _____

5 🎧 9.01 ⭐⭐ Listen again. Are the sentences T (true) or F (false)?

1 Emma and Mason can travel anywhere in Europe with their train tickets. __T__
2 Mason wants to go to the beach first. ____
3 Emma would like to visit museums. ____
4 Mason doesn't want to go to Finland because it's cold. ____
5 Mason would like to visit some European capitals. ____
6 Emma doesn't want to go to large cities. ____

UNIT 9 | A HOLIDAY ON THE MOON 75

LANGUAGE IN ACTION
Relative pronouns and relative clauses

1 ⭐ **Complete the sentences with relative pronouns.**
1. The town __where__ we went on holiday last year was quite cheap.
2. The plane _____ I took was two hours late.
3. Spring is the time of year _____ you can see beautiful pink trees in Japan.
4. The reason _____ I want to go to Turkey is to try the food.
5. The woman _____ suitcase was damaged was very upset.
6. New York is a good place for people _____ like sightseeing.

2 ⭐⭐ **Correct one mistake in each sentence.**
1. I remember where we went to London to see the Houses of Parliament.
   I remember when we went to London to see the Houses of Parliament.
2. This is the holiday resort I will be staying.
3. Is that the girl bag got lost?
4. I lost the camera I brought it with me.
5. I have an app on my phone tells me about all the best tourist attractions.
6. Mark is the person who I'm going to visit him in London.

3 ⭐⭐ **Complete the text with the clauses in the box and the correct relative pronouns.**

> brings you   has travelled to lots of countries
> I can see   I got a parcel in the post
> ~~I want to visit Japan~~   opinion I trust

The reason ¹_why I want to visit Japan_ is my brother Jonathan. He's someone ²_____, including the USA and Australia, but he always says that Japan is his favourite place. He was working there when I was quite young and he often used to send me presents. I loved the moment ³_____ and there was something inside, like a cool toy, food or a *maneki-neko* (this is like a little cat ⁴_____ good luck). So, Jonathan is the person ⁵_____ the most about travelling to different countries – I always ask him for advice. I hope I can visit Tokyo one day, and also other smaller towns ⁶_____ traditional Japanese life.

4 ⭐⭐⭐ **Join the sentences using a relative pronoun.**
1. These are the people. I met them on holiday.
   These are the people who I met on holiday.
2. France is the country. It has more tourists than any other country.
3. The departures lounge is a place in an airport. You wait for your plane there.
4. Drones are a new invention. They might replace normal taxis.
5. Norway is the place. I will be travelling there next summer.
6. We left early. The reason was bad weather.
7. Linda is the person. Her brother is a pilot.

76 A HOLIDAY ON THE MOON | UNIT 9

WRITING
An email to a host family

1 ⭐ Read the email quickly. Tick (✓) the information that Bedour wants to find out.

1. where Cardiff is
2. what she will study on the course
3. where she can find a place to stay
4. when the course starts
5. when the course finishes
6. how to travel to Cardiff

2 ⭐ Put a–e in the order they appear in Bedour's email (1–5).

a. ☐ goodbye
b. ☐ questions about the trip
c. [1] greeting
d. ☐ reason for writing
e. ☐ thanks

3 ⭐⭐ Complete the email with the *Useful language* phrases.

a. Best wishes
b. ~~Dear~~
c. Do you know
d. I'm writing to
e. thank you very much for

From: bedour2004@mymail.com
Subject: Summer course

¹ __Dear__ Mr Hamilton,

I hope you're well. ² _____ check some details of my visit to Cardiff this summer. I'm looking forward to starting the course and I hope I'm going to really improve my English!

As you may know, this is going to be my first time in the UK. Is it possible to ask some questions? I received your welcome pack which gives information about accommodation. Unfortunately, the places which were listed all look a long way from the centre of Cardiff. ³ _____ if I could find somewhere closer? I'd prefer not to spend too much time travelling each day.

I'd also like to ask about the exact dates of the course. I know the course will be starting on 25 June, but do I have to arrive earlier? Could you also tell me when the course ends, exactly? I'm asking because it's important for me to book my flights.

Finally, ⁴ _____ accepting me on this course. My family are all so happy for me!

⁵ _____,

Bedour

Write your own email to a school abroad.

PLAN

4 ⭐⭐ Decide what you are going to study and where. Write questions to ask your course organiser about these things.

Your travel plans and when you arrive

Your accommodation

Your course content and timetable

5 Decide what information to include. Use the information in Exercise 2 to help you.

WRITE

6 ⭐⭐⭐ Write your email. Remember to include *be going to*, the present continuous, the future continuous and phrases from the *Useful language* box (see Student's Book, p113).

CHECK

7 Do you …
- use a greeting at the beginning and say goodbye at the end?
- say why you are writing?
- say thank you?

UNIT 9 | A HOLIDAY ON THE MOON

9 REVIEW

VOCABULARY

1 **Match the beginnings of the sentences (1–8) with the ends (a–h).**

1 We arrived at our final
2 I didn't stay in my own country for my last holiday; I went
3 People like to visit the old market in my city – it's a popular
4 I stayed in a big
5 We went on several day
6 I went online and made all the
7 If I had lots of time, I'd like to
8 Hotels, hostels or villas: any

a trips to local towns.
b abroad.
c accommodation is OK for me.
d holiday resort and my room looked out over the beach.
e destination on time.
f go backpacking across the country.
g tourist attraction.
h bookings for my trip next week.

2 <u>Underline</u> and correct six travel phrasal verbs in the sentences.

1 You need to check on at the airport two hours before your flight. _____
2 Please check in of the hotel directly after breakfast, no later. _____
3 My plane gets in at five o'clock in the morning. I'm going to be so tired! _____
4 We're going out on holiday next week. Can you look after our cat? _____
5 My dad is on a business trip right now, but he'll get away tonight. _____
6 I looked on the city, but everything was closed. _____
7 After the plane took out, I had an amazing view from the window. _____
8 What time are you setting off for the airport tomorrow morning? _____

LANGUAGE IN ACTION

3 **Complete the sentences with the correct form of the verbs in the box. Use the tense in brackets.**

> have   live   meet   not learn   study   visit

1 Next week, I _____ lunch with my grandparents. (present continuous)
2 This time next year, I hope I _____ science at university. (future continuous)
3 Some people think that we _____ on other planets in the future. (future continuous)
4 We _____ lots of interesting places on holiday, I'm sure. (be going to)
5 My host family _____ me at the airport at six o'clock. (present continuous)
6 Emma _____ much Spanish; she's only staying in Madrid for two weeks. (be going to)

78 A HOLIDAY ON THE MOON | UNIT 9

4 Write sentences using the correct relative pronoun from the options in brackets.

1 The person was sitting near me on the plane is a famous actor! (who / which)

2 I stayed at a holiday resort is one of the best in the country. (why / which)

3 That's the passenger father is the pilot. (who / whose)

4 Cambodia is a country you can visit lots of interesting old cities. (where / that)

5 The main reason I want to visit Italy is all the great food. (which / why)

6 June and July is a time there's a lot of rain in Japan. (when / where)

CUMULATIVE LANGUAGE

5 Complete the text with the missing words. (Circle) the correct options.

Usually, it only takes about 12 hours to fly from the UK to Thailand. That's not ¹_____, but so far it's been 32 hours ²_____ I left home! I had set off for the airport early. I wanted to relax after checking in. After I ³_____ in, the first thing I saw on the screens was that my flight ⁴_____! At first, it was only two hours, then four, then eight! I ⁵_____ that there were problems with the aeroplane. It ⁶_____ in London yet. It was still in Moscow – about five hours away! The airline told me I ⁷_____ stay in a hotel near the airport and they would pay for it. At 3 am, I ⁸_____ a phone call saying that my plane had arrived, and that ⁹_____ I went immediately to the airport, I would miss the flight! I got on the plane and many hours later it landed at a new destination – Dhaka, the capital of Bangladesh! My plane needed ¹⁰_____ some other passengers. I'm still in Dhaka now! ¹¹_____ here for four hours so far! I ¹²_____ think that travelling was fun, but now I'm not so sure!

1 a long enough   b enough long   c too long
2 a since   b for   c from
3 a have checked   b check   c had checked
4 a was delayed   b delayed   c is delayed
5 a was told   b was said   c told
6 a hasn't arrived b didn't arrive   c hadn't arrived
7 a can   b could   c would
8 a get   b got   c was getting
9 a if   b when   c unless
10 a to pick up   b picking up   c pick up
11 a I was   b I've been   c I'd been
12 a used to   b use to   c did use to

EXAM TIPS: Reading skills

Reading: Multiple matching

Matching people with activities and things

You will read short descriptions of five people and match them with the best options. The options typically give information about places, services, entertainment, restaurants, etc.

There are eight options for five people, so there will be three extra. These extra options usually fit only partially.

Exam guide: Multiple matching

- To answer this question, you should first read through the short description of each person. You should then decide what the most important information about each one is and underline it.

- Before reading through the options, think about what sort of thing you would recommend for each person. For example, if they like eating fish, you might recommend a restaurant that specialises in fish dishes.

- Then read through each option and underline the important information.

- Always double-check and read the information carefully. Are there any traps? For example, a young man might be looking for a summer job on an organic farm and one of the options offers this. But beware! The young man also says he wants to improve his **French** and the job is in **Spain**, so it is not the perfect match.

- Be careful not to 'word spot'. If the same word is in the description and in one of the options, it might be a trap and not a match.

REMEMBER!

Make sure the text you choose matches all the requirements in the person's description.

Reading practice: Multiple matching

Synonyms

Tip!
The descriptions and the texts often have the same information, but they are written using different words.

1 **Read the text and match the words in bold with the words in the box.**

> accommodation   easy-going   famous   secretary
> said sorry   said we would   star   talk programme

I can really recommend the holiday ¹**apartment** in Pocos where we spent two weeks. The owner is a TV ²**celebrity** who has a popular late-night ³**chat show** and is very ⁴**well-known** in Brazil. We didn't meet her, but her ⁵**assistant** was waiting for us when we arrived. We ⁶**apologised** for being so late, but he was very friendly and ⁷**not at all difficult**. We ⁸**promised to** write a good review when we left!

1 _____   4 _____   7 _____
2 _____   5 _____   8 _____
3 _____   6 _____

Unknown words

2 Look at the word in bold in each sentence and choose the option you think has the closest meaning.

1 That actor played the **lead** in a film we went to see last week.
  A director   B hero   C role
2 Parents shouldn't be too **harsh** with teenagers at exam time.
  A strict   B proud   C miserable
3 This restaurant offers a wide **range** of vegetarian and vegan options.
  A variety   B line   C sort
4 He works with a team of exciting and **innovative** young designers.
  A athletic   B creative   C gentle

Tip! Sometimes you have to guess the meaning of a word you don't know. Look at the context by reading the sentences which come before and after the word.

Look out for traps

Tip! A useful way to check if your answer is correct is to think about why the other options are incorrect.

3 Read the descriptions of two people. Answer the questions.

A Gabriela wants to study English at a language school in Cambridge, where she has an aunt she can stay with. She loves football and wants to play in a team. Her language level is not very advanced, but she is very keen to learn. She wants small classes of mixed nationalities so that she has to speak English with her classmates.

B Winston is 25. He is very good at football and has played professionally. Now he wants to be a sports teacher, so he needs a teaching qualification in different sports. He is looking for a college outside a city with good sporting facilities and cheap college accommodation.

1 Which description mentions accommodation: A, B or both?
2 Which description mentions student accommodation: A, B or both?
3 Which person likes sport, especially football? Gabriela, Winston or both?
4 Which person wants to teach sport? Gabriela, Winston or both?

4 Read the descriptions of two colleges. Answer the questions.

Greystones College was built in 2003 in attractive open countryside just outside Oxford. Places are available for our language learning courses, which are taught in small numbers or intensively, one-to-one. Students stay with local families, to give them the greatest opportunities to practise their language skills. There are good sporting and social activities all year round.

Hinton College is located in one of the UK's oldest and most beautiful university cities and has a high level of success in English language learning. Our beginner classes are taught in groups of three or four by qualified native speakers. Social activities are arranged as part of the course and team sports are encouraged. All our courses are from one to six months in length.

1 <u>Underline</u> four important facts about each college:
   • where they are
   • what courses they offer
   • how big the classes are
   • what other activities they offer
2 What information tells you Greystones College is not suitable for Gabriela?
3 What information tells you Hinton College is suitable for Gabriela?

EXAM TIPS AND PRACTICE 81

EXAM TIPS: Writing skills

Writing an email in response to an annotated message

You will see a short message from an English-speaking friend. You have to respond to the message in around 100 words. This tests your ability to understand a message with notes and to write a clear response.

Exam guide: Writing an email

- Read the instructions carefully so that you understand who you are writing to and why you are writing.
- Your answer should be around 100 words. Don't write much more or much less than that.
- Begin and end your email correctly. Use:
  - your friend's name
  - an opening phrase
  - one sentences for each point from the original email
  - a phrase to close
  - your name at the end.
- Start your sentences in different ways to make your email interesting.
- Don't copy too much language from the question: try to think of synonyms where possible.

REMEMBER!

The message has handwritten notes which give you ideas about how to respond. You must use all the notes in your answer: you will lose marks if you don't!

Writing practice: Writing an email

1 Read the instructions and the statements that follow. Are the statements *T* (true) or *F* (false)?

You are planning to visit your friend Robin in Canada. Read Robin's message and the notes you have made on it. Then write an email to Robin.

	True	False
1 Your friend Robin is in Canada.	☐	☐
2 The message is from Robin.	☐	☐
3 Robin is planning to visit you.	☐	☐
4 The notes on the message are Robin's.	☐	☐
5 You answer using the notes.	☐	☐
6 Your answer should be in email form.	☐	☐

2 Read the sentences from two emails from the same boy. One is to his teacher, the other to his friend. Write them in the correct order under the right heading, formal or informal.

Formal	Informal

> **Tip!** Make sure you use the appropriate style: it should not be formal if you're writing to a friend.

I hope to be back at school on Monday.
I have a very bad cold and a high temperature.
Dear Mr Jacobs,
Yours, Michael Fanshaw
Please can you send me this week's homework?
I apologise for my absence from class yesterday.

Cheers, Mike
See you next week with any luck.
I've got an awful cold – I'm coughing and sweating.
Hi Pru,
Let me know if there's any homework, OK?
Sorry I wasn't there yesterday.

3 Change the words in **bold** to make the sentences more interesting. Use the words in the box or your own ideas.

> amazing   boring   brilliant   colourful   cool
> freezing   great   hate   love   pleasant   prefer   rainy

> **Tip!** Use a range of vocabulary: make sure you don't use the same word too many times.

1 There's a **good** skate park with a **good** café near my home.

2 We had a **nice** camping holiday but the weather was **not nice**.

3 I **like** swimming, but if you **don't like** it we can do something you'd **like more**.

4 The art galleries in my town are **not very interesting**, but the Museum of Tomorrow is **very interesting**.

5 We could go to the carnival: it's very **nice** and the costumes are usually **nice**.

4 Correct the mistake in each sentence.
1 Don't forget switch off the lights when you leave.

2 Are you scared thunder and lightning?

3 The weather forecast says it's going snowing tonight.

4 I can't sing because I've got a very hurt throat.

> **Tip!** Check your writing for any mistakes in spelling or grammar.

EXAM TIPS: Listening skills

Listening: Multiple choice

You will listen to short unrelated extracts and choose from three options. This tests your ability to listen for specific information and answer a question about what you hear.

Exam guide: Multiple choice

- Use the time before you listen to read the questions. Read them carefully because they tell you what you need to listen for.
- All the possible answers may be in the recording, but only one will answer the question.
- Focus on the general meaning of what you hear. You may have to listen for the person's opinion, which is not necessarily a single word or phrase.
- If you're not sure, mark the answers you think are possible and check on the second listening.
- Always give an answer, even if you're still not sure. A guess might be right.
- Use the second listening to check, even if you're sure you are right. Don't stop listening!

REMEMBER!

You will hear the instructions on the recording. Listen carefully and read the question at the same time because this will help you understand the topic and the context.

Listening practice: Multiple choice

1 Underline two key words or phrases in each question.
  1. What time does the girl's exam start?
  2. What is the man going to buy?
  3. Which evening activity is for beginners?
  4. Why did Caroline leave her job?
  5. Where are the teacher's keys?
  6. What did Hari do this morning?

Tip! Underline the key words in the question. Then listen for the words which mean the same as the key words.

2 (E.01) You will hear a teenage girl speaking to her mother about an exam. Read the question below.

What time does the girl's exam start?

A It starts at 11.30.
B Four o'clock.
C It begins at nine.

Now listen to the conversation. Why are options A and B not correct?

_____

Tip! If the recording is a dialogue, listen for the right person: who does the question refer to?

3 You will hear two people talking about a play they've just seen. What words do you expect to hear in connection with the three options? Choose from words in the box or use your own ideas.

> too long   too short   boring   interesting   bad
> great   impressive   old-fashioned

the length	the acting	the costumes

4 Listen to the conversation and answer the questions.
E.02
1 What did the woman think about the play?
   A She thought the play was too long.
   B She thought it was very disappointing.
   C She liked the actors.
2 What did the man think of the costumes?
   A He thought they were old-fashioned.
   B He likes fifties fashion.
   C He thought the clothes were terrible.
3 When is the play supposed to be set?
   A the 1950s
   B It's not mentioned.
   C nowadays

LANGUAGE REFERENCE

STARTER

Adverbs of frequency

Adverbs of frequency					
always	usually	often	sometimes	hardly ever	never
100%					0%

- We use **adverbs of frequency** to say how often something happens.
- We put them before the main verb, but after the verb **to be**.
  I often message my friends.
  There are always music festivals in summer.
- **Often, sometimes and usually** can also come at the beginning of the sentence.
  Sometimes, my family and I listen to music.

Expressions of frequency

every	day / week / weekend / year
once / twice / three times	a day / a week / a month / a year

- We also use **expressions of frequency** to say how often something happens.
- We usually place them after the verb phrase, but they can also come at the beginning or end of a sentence.
  I see my friends twice a week.
  Every weekend, they give a concert.
- We can use an expression of frequency and an adverb of frequency in the same sentence.
  I usually go on holiday once a year.

Present simple and present continuous

- We use the **present simple** to talk about facts, habits and routines.
  My sister likes rock music.   I use my phone every day.
- We use **adverbs of frequency** (*always*, *often*, etc.) with the **present simple** and *at the moment* and *now* with the **present continuous**.
  My dad often plays computer games with me.
  My teacher is walking into the classroom now.
- We also use the **present simple** to talk about future planned events if a **future time expression** is used or understood.
  My mum starts work at 10 am on Friday.
  Hannah can't come shopping with me this afternoon.

Past simple: regular and irregular verbs

	Affirmative	Negative
I / He / She / It We / You / They	called me.	didn't call me.

Question		
Did	I / he / she / it / we / you / they	call you?

Short answers			
Yes,	I / he / she / it / we / you / they	did.
No,	I / he / she / it / we / you / they	didn't.

- We use the **past simple** to talk about completed events and actions in the past.
  I watched the band play last night.
  Three years ago, she had a great party.
- To form the affirmative of the **past simple**, we add *-ed* or *-d* to the infinitive.
  help – helped   organise – organised   play – played
- For verbs ending **consonant + -y**, remove the *-y* and add *-ied*.
  study – studied   cry – cried   try – tried
- For verbs ending **consonant + vowel + consonant**, we double the final consonant and add *-ed*.
  drop – dropped   chat – chatted
- Many common verbs are irregular in the **past simple**.
  get – got   put – put
  have – had   make – made
- Question words always go at the beginning of the question.
  How did the fire start?
  Where was your brother last night?

LANGUAGE PRACTICE

STARTER

Present simple and present continuous with adverbs of frequency

1 Put the words in brackets in the correct place in the sentence.

1 Do you play in a band on Saturday night? (always)
   Do you always play in a band on Saturday night?
2 We see our friends at the jazz club in town. (sometimes)
3 My mum gets angry with me when I'm late. (never)
4 I text my teacher when I can't do my homework. (hardly ever)
5 My brother's football team wins the cup. (often)
6 Are those music apps free or not? (usually)

2 Complete the sentences with the correct form of the verbs in the box.

do   go   have   ~~post~~   spend   study

1 *Does* your sister usually *post* photos on social media?
2 I'm on holiday at the moment and I _____ a great time!
3 How much money _____ you usually _____ each week?
4 What _____ your parents _____ when you get good grades at school?
5 We _____ by bus today because it's too cold to walk.
6 She _____ for exams this weekend, so she hasn't got much free time.

Present simple for future

3 Put the words in the correct order to make sentences about the future.

1 eight / English / at / starts / lesson / past / Our / half
   Our English lesson starts at half past eight.
2 begin / time / the / does / tomorrow / What / concert / ?
3 arrives / at / train / My / 6.40 / grandparents'
4 six / This / phone / shuts / tonight / mobile / at / shop
5 the trip / We / for / morning / leave / our / in / early
6 back / teacher / week / We / our / next / essays / the / get / from

Past simple

4 Use the prompts to make questions and answers in the past simple.

1 When / you see that film? / last week
   When did you see that film? I/We saw it last week.
2 What time / the girls go to bed? / after 11
3 Where / your parents meet? / at college
4 What / he buy yesterday? / a new bike
5 How / the visitors get here? / by boat
6 When / the last bus leave? / at ten

LANGUAGE REFERENCE

UNIT 1

Past continuous

	Affirmative	Negative
I / He / She / It	was crying.	wasn't crying.
We / You / They	were crying.	weren't crying.
Questions		
Was	I / he / she / it	crying?
Were	we / you / they	
Short answers		
Yes,	I / he / she / it	was.
	we / you / they	were.
No,	I / he / she / it	wasn't.
	we / you / they	weren't.

- We use the **past continuous** to talk about actions in progress around a time in the past.
  At seven o'clock, I was waiting for the bus.
  Chloe was wearing jeans yesterday.
- We also use **when**, **while** and **as** to mean 'during that time' or to connect two events happening at the same time.
  When my parents were studying, they didn't have the internet.
  While he was eating, the phone rang.
  As Heather was walking, she was singing a song.

used to

	Affirmative	Negative
I / He / She / It	used to play football.	didn't use to play football.
We / You / They		
Questions and short answers		
Did	I / you / he / she / it / we / you / they use to be scared?	
Yes,	I / he / she / it / we / you / they	did.
No,		didn't.

- **Used to** emphasises that past states, habits and actions are now finished.
  It used to be a library, but now it's a museum.
  We used to walk to school, but now we cycle.
- We do not use **used to** to talk about things that only happened once, how many times something happened or duration.
  They went to the cinema yesterday.
  ~~They used to go to the cinema yesterday.~~
  My brother lived there for four years.
  ~~My brother used to live there for four years.~~
- **Used to** does not have a present form. For present habits and states, we use the present simple.
  My cousin drinks coffee in the morning.

LANGUAGE PRACTICE

UNIT 1

Past simple and past continuous with *when*, *while* and *as*

1 Complete the sentences with the past continuous form of the verbs in the box.

> cook   look   ~~snow~~   not study   wear

1 It __was snowing__ all day yesterday, so we didn't play football.
2 We _____ for you after class. Where were you?
3 Yanis _____ – he was reading a magazine!
4 Nina _____ her new shoes for the first time.
5 What _____ you _____ in the kitchen earlier? It didn't smell very nice!

2 Write sentences with *when*, *while* or *as* and the correct form of the verbs. Some sentences can have more than one answer.

1 Her father / wait / she arrive home
   Her father was waiting when she arrived home.
2 The doorbell / ring / I make tea
3 The boys / cycle home / their teacher drive past
4 Our friends / arrive / we prepare lunch
5 I / listen to music / I do my homework

3 Circle the correct option.

1 What *did they do* / (*were they doing*) when (*we called*) / *were calling* them?
2 She *watched* / *was watching* a film when her computer *broke* / *was breaking*.
3 I *didn't see* / *wasn't seeing* you while I *shopped* / *was shopping* in town.
4 The police *stopped* / *were stopping* her when she *drove* / *was driving* to work.
5 We *walked* / *were walking* to school when the rain *started* / *was starting*.
6 They *shouted* / *were shouting* for ages, but nobody *heard* / *was hearing* them.

4 Complete the conversation with the correct past form of the verbs in brackets.

KARIM   Hi, Lena! ¹ __Did you finish__ (you / finish) your history essay yesterday?
LINA   No, I ² _____ (work) on it after school when my mum ³ _____ (stop) me.
KARIM   Why ⁴ _____ (she / do) that?
LINA   Because she ⁵ _____ (want) me to help her with dinner. Then my brother and I ⁶ _____ (watch) a wildlife film on TV.
KARIM   Oh yeah, I ⁷ _____ (see) that! So then I guess you ⁸ _____ (be) too tired!
LINA   Correct!

used to

5 Make sentences with the correct form of *used to* and the verbs in the box.

> not eat   ~~have~~   live   play

1 Our neighbours __used to have__ a horse.
2 We _____ in a smaller apartment.
3 Children _____ outside until it got dark.
4 Ollie _____ vegetables, but he does now.

6 Make questions to match the answers.

1 *Did you use to go to school by bus* ?
   No, not by bus. I went to school by bike.
2 _____ ?
   No, my sister's never eaten meat.
3 _____ ?
   No, my sister played with me, but not my brother.
4 _____ ?
   Olives? No, and I still hate them!

7 Circle the correct options.

British schoolteachers in the 1950s ¹(*used to write*) / *used writing* on chalkboards because, of course, they ² *didn't have* / *weren't having* today's technology. They ³ *used to talk* / *did talk* a lot while the children ⁴ *were sitting* / *didn't sit* quietly. School books never ⁵ *didn't use to look* / *looked* very interesting and there weren't any videos to watch. Many teachers ⁶ *used to be* / *were being* stricter than they are now, too.

LANGUAGE REFERENCE

UNIT 2

Present perfect: regular verbs

Affirmative / Negative			Questions		
I / We / You / They	have walked / haven't walked	to school.	Have	I / we / you / they	walked to school?
He / She / It	has walked / hasn't walked		Has	he / she / it	
Short answers					
Yes,	I / we / you / they	have.	No,	I / we / you / they	haven't.
	he / she / it	has.		he / she / it	hasn't.

- We use the **present perfect** to talk about actions, experiences and facts in the past, when the exact time is not mentioned or important.
  The orchestra have played my favourite song.
  He has visited the art exhibition.

- We form the affirmative with **subject + have/has + past participle**.
  I've talked to Danielle.   She's asked me for help.

- We form the negative with **subject + haven't/hasn't + past participle**.
  Max hasn't auditioned for the part.
  They haven't performed in front of an audience.

- We form questions in the **present perfect** with *have/has + subject + past participle*. We often use *ever* in present perfect questions to ask about your whole life.
  Has she ever had drum lessons?
  Have you ever been to the theatre?

- We often use *never* to say 'not at any time' when answering these questions.
  A: Has he ever met a famous person?   B: No, never.

- Regular past participles end in *-ed, -d* or *-ied*.
  want – wanted   believe – believed   worry – worried

Present perfect: irregular verbs

- Many common verbs have irregular past participles.
  go – gone   put – put   be – been   make – made
  see – seen   hear – heard

- We use *go (gone)* to say somebody has not returned from a place or from doing an activity. We use *be (been)* to say somebody has returned from a place or from doing an activity.
  They've gone to Rome. (They are in Paris now.)
  They've been to Rome. (They have returned.)

Present perfect with *just*

- We use *just* with the present perfect to talk about very recent events and actions.
  I've just heard the good news. It's fantastic!
  Dad's just got home and he's feeling tired.

Present perfect with *already*, *still* and *yet*

- We often use *already*, *still* and *yet* with the present perfect.
  Jack has already been to the exhibition twice.
  We still haven't chosen a film to watch.
  I haven't had time to go shopping yet.

- We use *already* to explain that something happened before we expected or to emphasise it has happened. We normally put *already* between *have* and the **past participle**.
  She has already bought a ticket. I have already seen the show.

- We use *still* in negative sentences to express that something we expected has not happened but we imagine it will happen in the future. We put *still* directly after the subject.
  My uncle still hasn't seen the new play.

- We use *yet* in negative sentences to emphasise that something we expected has not happened. We put *yet* after the complete verb phrase.
  John hasn't arrived yet.
  I haven't asked my parents for permission yet.

- We use *yet* in questions to ask if something has happened before now. It comes at the end of the question.
  Have you bought the bus tickets yet?

- In short answers in the negative, we say **Not yet**.
  A: Have you spoken to the drama teacher? B: Not yet.

LANGUAGE PRACTICE

UNIT 2

Present perfect with regular and irregular verbs

1 Complete the sentences with the present perfect form of the verbs in brackets.
1. A TV celebrity __has opened__ (open) a new supermarket in our town.
2. This Chinese circus _____ (not perform) in Europe before.
3. I _____ (look) everywhere, but I can't find my phone.
4. _____ the DJ _____ (play) your favourite song?
5. Our teacher _____ (work) as a film-maker.
6. _____ they _____ (invite) you to their exhibition?

2 Complete the sentences with been or gone.
1. We've _been_ on holiday. We came home yesterday.
2. Felix has _____ to Brazil three times.
3. The children have _____ out, but they won't be late.
4. I've _____ shopping. Please help me with my bags.
5. Where's Jared? Has he _____ to bed?
6. My mum's not here. She's _____ to work.

3 Write questions with the present perfect and the phrases in the box. Then write true answers.

> be to a science museum   take music lessons
> make a sculpture   see a ballet   win a prize

1. Have you ever been to a science museum?
   Yes, I have. / No, I haven't.
2.
3.
4.
5.
6.

Present perfect with *just*, *already*, *still*, and *yet*

4 Put the words in the correct order.
1. written / I've / some / lyrics / just / cool
   I've just written some cool lyrics.
2. *Hamlet* / seen / a / just / of / She's / performance
3. song / We / just / our / first / recorded / have
4. the / started / just / They've / rehearsal
5. auditioned / a / for / show / a / just / Mina / has / part / in

5 Circle the correct sentences.
1. A (She still hasn't played in a professional orchestra.)
   B She yet hasn't played in a professional orchestra.
2. A The concert tickets haven't arrived yet.
   B The concert tickets haven't arrived still.
3. A Have you read this review? No, already not.
   B Have you read this review? No, not yet.
4. A Janek has already seen that film twice.
   B Janek has still seen that film twice.

6 Put the words in brackets in the correct position in the sentences.
1. Esma has heard from the film director. (just)
   Esma has just heard from the film director.
2. Has she had her audition? (yet)
3. Yes, she's had an audition and an interview (already).
4. Has she heard what part she's got? (yet)
5. No, the director hasn't told her. (still)

LANGUAGE REFERENCE

UNIT 3

can, could, will be able to

- We often use **can** to talk about ability to do something in the present.
  She can speak English and Polish.
- We often use **could** to talk about ability to do something in the past.
  We could visit the pyramids when we went to Egypt.
- We often use **will be able to** to talk about ability to do something in the future.
  I will be able to translate this document tomorrow.

Present perfect with *for/since* and *How long ... ?*

For and since

- We use **for** and **since** with the **present perfect** to say how long something has been true.
  She hasn't lived in Manchester for three years.
  I've lived here since I was seven.
- We use **for** with periods of time.
  Liam's had a new bike for three days.
  My parents have been married for 21 years.
- We use **since** with a reference to a specific time.
  We've been best friends since 2009.
  Emma and Anna haven't seen each other since June.

How long ... ?

- We use **How long ...?** + **present perfect** to ask about the duration of a state or activity.
  A: *How long have you known Greg?*
  B: *I've known him since 2012.*

Present perfect and past simple

- We use the **past simple** when the moment in which something happened has ended. When it happened isn't always mentioned, usually because it is clear.
  I went to Liverpool in June. (it's now July)
  They began the exam two minutes ago. (it's now 10.02, not 10.00)
  She wanted to ask you a question. (when I spoke to her)
- We use the **present perfect** when something started or happened in the past and continues to be true until now. We can say how long something has been true, but not when it started.
  I've been to Liverpool. (when isn't specified, but it continues to be true)
  They've begun the exam. (and the exam hasn't finished)
  She's wanted to ask you a question for a few days. (she continues to want to)

LANGUAGE PRACTICE

UNIT 3

can, could, will be able to

1 Are the sentences about the *P* (past), *Pr* (present) or *F* (future)?
1 We won't be able to wave goodbye when they leave. __F__
2 I can translate the instructions for you. ____
3 He will be able to come to the meeting. ____
4 My parents couldn't understand their Turkish guests. ____
5 She couldn't hear her phone, so she didn't answer. ____
6 We can't wait or we'll miss our bus. ____

2 Complete the text with the correct form of *can*, *could* or *will be able to*.

> Beatriz comes from São Paulo, so she ¹ __can__ speak Brazilian Portuguese very well. She speaks English fairly well, but she ² _____ always understand if people talk too fast. When she was younger, she ³ _____ speak Spanish, but she studied it at school and now she ⁴ _____ . Next year, she's going to stay with an aunt in Luzern. She ⁵ _____ learn Swiss German there, but she ⁶ _____ understand people in the French and Italian speaking regions of the country.

3 Circle the correct options.
1 We ____ hear the speaker because he's talking quietly.
  A could B couldn't C (can't)
2 Hamza is so good at languages. He ____ speak a lot of them!
  A will be able to B could C can
3 My parents ____ choose to learn Greek or Latin when they were at school.
  A could B can C can't
4 I hope I ____ help you later. I'll be free this evening.
  A can't B will be able to C could
5 We ____ see the video if we miss the next class.
  A couldn't B won't be able to C can to
6 ____ visit the British Museum when you're in London next week?
  A Able you to B Can you able to C Will you be able to

Present perfect with for/since and How long ... ?

4 Complete the sentences with *for* or *since*.
1 I have known my friend Victoria __for__ four years.
2 She hasn't seen her grandparents _____ a long time.
3 We've lived in this apartment _____ 2010.
4 Have you been at home _____ lunchtime?

5 Make questions with *How long* and the correct form of the verb.
1 you / be at this school?
  How long have you been at this school?
2 she / know her best friend?
  _____
3 they / live near you?
  _____
4 Lucas / have that phone?
  _____

Present perfect and past simple

6 Circle the correct options.
1 My mother (has worked) / worked at this museum since 2004.
2 He *has told* / *told* me the same joke yesterday.
3 They *haven't begun* / *didn't begin* the exam yet.
4 *Has she ever told* / *Did she ever tell* lies before?

7 Complete the conversation with the correct form of the verbs in brackets.

LUIS Sorry I'm late, Vlad. How long ¹ __have you been__ (be) here?
VLAD No problem, I ² _____ (just get) here.
LUIS ³ _____ the teacher _____ (arrive) yet?
VLAD No, not yet. She ⁴ _____ (tell) us yesterday that she might be late.
LUIS Oh, did she? I ⁵ _____ (not hear) that. Your English is very good!
VLAD Thanks! I ⁶ _____ (study) it since 5th grade.

LANGUAGE REFERENCE & PRACTICE 93

LANGUAGE REFERENCE

UNIT 4

Quantifiers

Countable	Uncountable
a few	a little
enough	enough
too many	too much

- We use **quantifiers** to talk about the amount of something.
- We use **a few** and **a little** to express small quantities.
  I've got a few messages that I need to reply to.
  I have a little time to watch TV, but not much.
- We use **too many**/**too much** to say that an amount is excessive.
  There were too many options. I didn't know what to choose!
  There was too much noise and I couldn't sleep.
- We use **enough** to say that a quantity is sufficient and **not enough** to say that a quantity is insufficient.
  We've got enough players to make two teams.
  I didn't have enough time to answer all the questions.

should/shouldn't/ought to

	Affirmative	Negative
I / He / She / It	should help.	shouldn't help.
We / You / They		
Questions		
Should	I / he / she / it / we / you / they	help?
Short answers		
Yes,	I / he / she / it / we / you / they	should.
No,		shouldn't.

- We use **should** to say what we think is a good idea or important to do – to give advice and recommendations.
  You should stay in bed if you have a fever.
  Laura shouldn't use her phone before bed.
- **Should** is the same in all forms. We use an infinitive without **to** after **should**.
  John should get more sleep. (John ~~should to get~~ more sleep.)
- We use **ought to** when talking about things which are desired or ideal.
  We ought to eat lots of fruit and vegetables every day.

LANGUAGE PRACTICE

UNIT 4

Quantifiers

1 Match the beginnings of the sentences with the ends.
1 Please be quiet, there's
2 Too many students
3 Yoga exercises don't take
4 You'll be tired if you have
5 Do you think there's
6 Muscles get weak if you spend

a too much time, do they?
b too many late nights.
c too many hours sitting at a desk!
d too much noise in here.
e are worried about their exams.
f too much stress in your life?

2 Complete the sentences with *a little* or *a few*.
1 I do _a few_ yoga exercises every morning at 7 am.
2 Jorge can give you _____ help in the gym if you need it.
3 There are _____ adjustable desks in our classroom.
4 You should take _____ exercise during long study sessions.
5 Karla needs _____ more time to finish her homework.
6 Stop working for _____ minutes and take a walk.

3 Put the words in the correct order.
1 the / time / didn't / We / to / test / have / enough / finish
   We didn't have enough time to finish the test.
2 bike / enough / buy / Gisela's / to / a / money / new / got
   _____
3 team / make / There / students / a / are / enough / to
   _____
4 drive / old / you / car / Are / a / enough / to / ?
   _____
5 me / adjustable / enough / This / high / isn't / desk / for
   _____

4 Circle the correct option.
1 (A few) / A little new students joined our swimming class.
2 I've got *time enough* / *enough time* to help you.
3 These desks cost *too much* / *too many* money.
4 There were *a little* / *a few* problems we couldn't solve.
5 Has everyone got *too much* / *too many* stress in their lives?
6 Emilio takes *a little* / *a few* exercise but not much.

should/shouldn't/ought to

5 Complete the sentences with *should*, *shouldn't* or *ought*.
1 You _shouldn't_ worry about the test – it'll be easy!
2 Melody _____ to go to bed early and get more sleep.
3 _____ Paula stay at home if she's feeling ill?
4 I _____ to have more fish, but I don't really like it.
5 We _____ buy too many sweet things – they're bad for our teeth.

6 Correct the mistake in each sentence.
1 We ~~shouldn't~~ take our coats today because it's really cold.
   We should take our coats today because it's really cold.
2 Bella ought be more easygoing: she worries too much.
   _____
3 You should to stay in bed if you have a fever.
   _____
4 Who should I to ask when I need advice?
   _____
5 We shouldn't all drink enough water.
   _____

7 Complete the text with the phrases in the box.

| ought to ask   ought to do   should find |
| should listen   ~~should read~~   should speak |
| shouldn't start   shouldn't worry |

Top tips for improving your English

You [1] _should read_ English language magazines or websites. You [2] _____ this as often as possible. If you like reading, you [3] _____ English books or stories, but you [4] _____ your teacher for recommendations. You [5] _____ with something that's too difficult. You [6] _____ to as much English as possible too: podcasts, radio and TV are all good.

LANGUAGE REFERENCE   UNIT 5

First conditional

if- clause	Main clause
(*if* + present simple)	(*will/won't, may/might* (*not*), *could*)
If I pass all my exams,	my parents will / may / might buy me a present.
If I don't pass all my exams, Unless I pass all my exams,	I won't / may not / might not go on holiday.

Main clause	*if*- clause
(*will/won't, may/might* (*not*), *could*)	(*if* + present simple)
My parents will / may / might buy me a present	if I pass my exams.
My parents won't buy me a present	if I don't pass all my exams. unless I pass all my exams.

Question	
Will my parents buy me a present	if I don't pass all my exams?

- We use **first conditional** sentences to talk about possible situations in the present or future and say what we think the result will be.
- We often use ***if* + present simple** to describe the possible action or event.
  We'll pass the exam if we work hard.
- We can use **unless + present simple** instead of *if not*.
  Unless we hurry up, we'll miss the train.
- We use ***will/won't* + infinitive** when we are sure of the result and ***may*** or ***might* + infinitive** when we are less sure.
  If we don't leave now, we won't catch the 8:30 bus.
  If my grandfather doesn't feel better, he may not visit this weekend.
  I might go the beach if it's warm enough.
- When we use *if* to start the sentence, we use a comma between the two parts.
  If I've got enough money, I'll go on holiday.
- We normally use ***will*** to make first conditional questions. It is unusual to use ***may*** or ***might***.
  Will you chat with me online this evening if you have time?

Second conditional

if- clause	Main clause
(*if* + present simple)	(*would/could/might* + infinitive)
If I knew him,	I would / could / might ask him.
If I didn't know him,	I wouldn't / couldn't / might not ask him.

Main clause	*if*- clause
(*would/could/might* + infinitive)	(*if* + past simple)
I would / could / might ask him	if I knew him.
I wouldn't / couldn't / might not ask him	if I didn't know him.

Question	
Would you ask him	if you knew him?

- We use the **second conditional** to talk about imaginary situations in the present and their possible consequences.
- We use ***if* + past simple** (affirmative or negative) to describe the imaginary situation and ***would***, ***could*** or ***might*** for the consequence.
  If he didn't like you, he wouldn't talk to you.
- We use ***would*** (***not***) when we are sure of the consequence.
  He would do better in school if he didn't spend all his time playing computer games.
- We use ***could*** (***not***) to express a possibility or ability as a consequence.
  If it was Saturday, we could go out for pizza.
  I could do some volunteer work if I didn't need to study so much.
- We use ***might*** (***not***) to show we are less sure about the consequence.
  If I had more free time, I might take up the guitar.
  Madison might lend you her laptop if you asked her.
- We can use ***was*** or ***were*** in the *if*- part of the sentence with *I, he/she* and *it*.
  If it wasn't/weren't so spicy, I could finish it.
  I wouldn't say anything if I were/was you.

LANGUAGE PRACTICE

UNIT 5

First conditional

1 Circle the correct option.
1 If I *have* / *will have* enough time, I'll help you pick up litter.
2 Unless Jenny calls, *we don't know* / *won't know* where she is.
3 Many more fish will die if they *eat* / *will eat* our plastic waste.
4 *If* / *Unless* we use solar power, we will reduce air pollution.
5 We might go swimming later if the sun *comes* / *will come* out.

2 Put the phrases in the correct order.
1 I might / I have enough money, / If / buy a new phone
   If I have enough money, I might buy a new phone.
2 come to school later / you feel better / if / Will you / ?
3 if / Henry will / he leaves last / switch off the lights
4 climate change, / our planet / Unless / we stop / will get hotter
5 we'll miss / we don't leave soon, / the beginning of the film / If
6 we collect all the plastic / The ocean / if / might get cleaner

Second conditional

3 Choose the correct words to complete the sentences.
1 Our planet would be in danger if all the insects *would disappear* / *disappeared*.
2 What *would you do* / *did you do* if someone gave you a plastic straw?
3 Where *would you travel* / *would you travelled* if you had enough money?
4 There would be more oxygen if they *wouldn't destroy* / *didn't destroy* rainforests.
5 We could reduce the effects of climate change if we *would use* / *used* solar power.

4 Complete the second conditional sentences with the correct form of the words in brackets.
1 If I *had* (have) the answer to the problems of climate change, I *would tell* (tell) you.
2 She _____ (not ask) you to come if she _____ (not like) you.
3 We _____ (not endanger) animals so much if we _____ (not destroy) their habitats.
4 If we _____ (live) near the sea, I think our home _____ (be) in danger.
5 I _____ (not eat) meat if I _____ (be) you.

5 Correct the mistake in each sentence.
1 What would you do if you had won a million euros?
   What would you do if you won a million euros?
2 If you didn't work so hard you would get so stressed.
3 Would those animals safer if they lived in a zoo?
4 I didn't eat fish unless I lived near the sea.

6 Write second conditional sentences about the problems.
1 I haven't got enough money to buy a new phone
   have more money / buy a new phone
   If I had more money, I would buy a new phone.
2 This coffee isn't sweet enough.
   this coffee / be better / if / you add / a little sugar to it
3 We're not healthy because the air is polluted.
   we all / be healthier / if / the air / not polluted
4 There are enough insects to feed everybody.
   if / we all / eat insects / nobody / be hungry

LANGUAGE REFERENCE

UNIT 6

Present simple passive

Affirmative			Negative	
This bottle	is	made of plastic.	isn't	made of plastic.
These toys	are		aren't	
Questions			Short answers	
Is	this bottle	made of plastic?	Yes,	it is.	No,	it isn't.
Are	these toys			they are.		they aren't.

- We use the **passive** form to describe actions and processes when we are not interested in, or don't know, who is responsible for the action or process.
  English is spoken in many countries.
  Many plastic bottles aren't recycled.
- To form the **present simple passive**, we use *is/are* (*not*) + **past participle**.
  The streets are cleaned on Sundays after the market finishes.
- We form questions with *Is/Are* + **subject** + **past participle**.
  Is the main square decorated during the festival?
  When are the results sent to students?

Past simple passive

Affirmative			Negative	
The rubbish	was	thrown away.	wasn't	thrown away.
The old chairs	were		weren't	
Questions			Short answers	
Was	the rubbish	thrown away?	Yes,	it was.	No,	it wasn't.
Were	the old chairs			they were.		they weren't.

- We use the **past simple passive** to describe actions and processes in the past.
  The competition winners were given books and a certificate.
- To form the **past simple passive**, we use *was/were* (*not*) + **past participle**.
  The first CD was made in 1982.
  Some of us weren't invited to the party.
- To form questions, we use *was/were* + **subject** + **past participle**.
  Were the instructions written in Spanish or Portuguese?

Passive + *by*

- We use *by* with the **passive** to show who or what was responsible for the action.
  The 'Merchant of Venice' was written by Shakespeare.
  A lot of houses were destroyed by the fire.

LANGUAGE PRACTICE

UNIT 6

Present simple passive

1 Complete the conversation with the present simple passive form of the verbs in brackets.

ANA How much waste [1] _is recycled_ (recycle) in your home?

BEN Well, glass and metal [2] _____ (collect) every week. I'm not sure what [3] _____ (do) with other materials we recycle. Some waste [4] _____ (burn).

ANA Yes, but burning waste isn't great. The air [5] _____ (pollute) because dangerous gases like methane [6] _____ (create).

BEN True, but you can do simple things to help. I never buy fruit that [7] _____ (pack) in plastic and very little energy [8] _____ (waste) in our apartment.

2 Complete the text with the present simple passive form of the verbs in the box.

> eat   fly   not grow   pack   process
> produce   sell   send

A lot of the food that [1] _is eaten_ in the UK [2] _____ there. Oranges, for example, [3] _____ in California. They [4] _____ there and then they [5] _____ to airports in Europe. Lorries transport the fruit to towns, where they [6] _____ in supermarkets. Incredibly, some food [7] _____ by ship to China, where it [8] _____ before returning to Europe.

3 Circle the correct option to complete the sentences.

1. Where _____ BMW cars _____ ?
   A did … produce   B (are … produced)
   C produced … by

2. The equipment _____ in a small factory near here.
   A is pack   B packed   C is packed

3. A very strong tape _____ these boxes.
   A is secured   B secures   C are secured

4. Their work _____ every day by the managers.
   A inspects   B is inspecting   C is inspected

5. The end product _____ for many different things.
   A uses   B is used   C has used

Past simple passive

4 Complete the sentences with the past simple passive form of the verbs in brackets.

1. The frisbee _was invented_ (invent) by American college students.
2. The Shard _____ (build) near the river in London.
3. My favourite picture _____ (paint) by Frida Kahlo.
4. The factory workers _____ (not pay) very much.
5. English _____ (speak) in many holiday resorts.

5 Write questions using the past simple passive.

1. what clothes / wear / by teenagers in the 1950s
   What clothes were worn by teenagers in the 1950s?
2. who / that amazing building / design by
   _____
3. where / the American soldiers / send
   _____
4. what / those old wooden boxes / use for
   _____

6 Answer the questions in Exercise 5. Use the information given.

1. blue jeans and T-shirts
   Blue jeans and T-shirts were worn by teenagers in the 1950s.
2. Frank Lloyd Wright
   _____
3. to Europe
   _____
4. packing equipment
   _____

7 Rewrite the questions using the past simple passive with *by*.

Who found those beautiful cave paintings?
   Who were those beautiful cave paintings found by?

2. What destroyed the city of Pompeii?
   _____
3. Who wrote *Romeo and Juliet*?
   _____
4. Who built Machu Picchu?
   _____

LANGUAGE REFERENCE & PRACTICE 99

LANGUAGE REFERENCE

UNIT 7

Past perfect

Affirmative				Negative	
I / You / He / She / It	had forgotten.	I / You / He / She / It	hadn't (had + not) forgotten.		
We / You / They		We / You / They			
Questions			Short answers		
Had	I / you / he / she / it	forgotten?	Yes,	I / you / he / she / it	had.
	we / you / they		No,	we / you / they	hadn't.

- We use the **past perfect** with other past tenses to talk about actions or states that happened before the main past action or state.
  We hadn't seen the news, so we didn't know about the storms.
  I couldn't call you on Friday because I had left my phone at home.

Reported statements

	Direct speech	Reported speech
Present simple	'I **want** some new jeans'.	He said (that) he **wanted** some new jeans.
Present continuous	'We**'re making** our own clothes'.	He said (that) they **were making** their own clothes.
Past simple	'I **had** a great time'.	She said (that) she**'d had** a great time.
Present perfect	'We**'ve just seen** a live concert'.	She said (that) they**'d just** seen a live concert.

- When we report somebody's words, we often have to change the verb forms – see the table above for how the verb forms change.
- We often need to change pronouns in reported speech.
  '<u>You</u> have to arrive before 7 pm'. – He said (that) <u>we</u> had to arrive before 7 pm.

LANGUAGE PRACTICE

UNIT 7

Past perfect

1 Complete the sentences with the past perfect form of the verbs in brackets.
1. I couldn't go to the performance because I ____had been____ (be) ill.
2. She _____ (not sleep) very well, so she felt tired all day.
3. I was happy because my team _____ (win).
4. We realised that we _____ (meet) once before.
5. He _____ (know) about the event for a long time.

2 Circle the correct option.
1. When we arrived, the street party _____
   A already was started. B has already started.
   C (had already started)
2. I didn't want to see the movie until I _____ the book.
   A was read   B had read   C hadn't read
3. When we heard the noise, we knew something _____
   A had happened.   B happened.   C happens.
4. They were so late that the performance _____
   A has nearly finished.   B nearly had finished.
   C had nearly finished.
5. Yolanda ran to the station but the train _____
   A had just leave.   B had just left.
   C was just left.

Reported statements

3 Circle the correct option.
1. They (say)/tell that it's the biggest carnival in the world.
2. Edwin said/told everyone that he wasn't coming.
3. Did anyone say/tell you what time the film began?
4. I have already said/told you not to do that.
5. The ticket says/tells that costumes are optional.

4 Write the direct speech in reported speech.
1. 'I had an interesting holiday.'
   He said (that) _he'd had an interesting holiday._
2. 'I've already read the film review.'
   Maria said (that) _____.
3. 'We're making pizzas for dinner.'
   They said (that) _____.
4. 'Juan can't leave before eight.'
   I told them (that) _____.

5 Write the reported speech in direct speech.
1. She said she'd booked tickets for the exhibition.
   'I've booked tickets for the exhibition.'
2. He told me he didn't watch any daytime TV.
   _____.
3. Jacky said she was waiting for her friend to arrive.
   _____.
4. We told them we had never heard that band.
   _____.

6 Read the email. Then complete the reported speech below.

Home | Inbox | Sent | New

Hi Diana,
Bernie and I are having a brilliant time in Rio! We're staying near the Copacabana beach, so we've swum every day. The carnival has been amazing. I've never seen so many fabulous costumes. We've loved every minute! Actually, we don't want to leave!
Love, Susie

I've just had an email from Susie, who's in Rio with Bernie. She said they ¹ ____were having____ a brilliant time. She said they ² _____ near the Copacabana beach, so they ³ _____ every day. She wrote that the carnival ⁴ _____ amazing. She said that she ⁵ _____ so many fabulous costumes. She told me that they ⁶ _____ every minute. Actually, they ⁷ _____ to leave!

LANGUAGE REFERENCE

UNIT 8

can/can't, be allowed to

Affirmative/Negative	
I'm (not)	
You / We / They're (not)	allowed to run.
He / She / It's (not)	

Questions			Short answers
Am	I	allowed to run?	Yes, I am. No, I'm not.
Are	you / we / they		Yes, you / we / they are. No, you / we / they aren't.
Is	he / she / it		Yes, he / she / it is. No, he / she / it isn't.

- We use **be allowed to** to say that we have permission to do something.
  We're allowed to use my aunt's laptop.
  You're not allowed to take these books out of the library.
- We often contract **be** in negative sentences.
  They aren't allowed to have phones in class.
  He isn't allowed to go to the party.

must/mustn't

Affirmative		Negative
I / He / She / It We / You / They	must go.	mustn't go.

- We use **must** to say what we think it is necessary to do, to talk about obligation and to give strong recommendations.
  I must start studying more.
  You must listen to this song. It's fantastic!
- We use **mustn't** to say what we think it is necessary not to do, to talk about prohibition and to give strong advice against something.
  We mustn't forget to buy her a present.
  Tell them that they mustn't be late tomorrow.
- Questions with **must** are not very common as they sound quite formal. We tend to use **have to** instead.
  Must I go to bed so early? Do I have to go to bed so early?
- **Must** is the same in all forms.
- We use an infinitive without **to** after **must**.

need to/don't need to

Affirmative		Negative
I / We / You / They	need to work.	don't need to work.
He / She / It	needs to work.	doesn't need to work.

Questions		
Do	I / we / you / they	need to work?
Does	he / she / it	

Short answers					
Yes,	I / we / you / they	do.	No,	I / we / you / they	don't.
	he / she / it	does.		he / she / it	doesn't.

- We use **need** to say that there is an obligation to do something.
  I need to go home after class.
- We use **don't need to** to say there is no obligation to do something.
  I don't need to take the bus. I can walk.

have to/don't have to

Affirmative / Negative	
I / We / You / They	have to learn / don't have to learn.
He / She / It	has to learn / doesn't have to learn.

Questions		
Do	I / we / you / they	have to learn?
Does	he / she / it	

Short answers					
Yes,	I / we / you / they	do.	No,	I / we / you / they	don't.
	he / she / it	does.		he / she / it	doesn't.

- We use **have to** to say what it is necessary to do.
  You have to answer all the questions in the exam.
  He has to wear a uniform at school.
- We use **don't have to** to say that it is not necessary to do something, but that you can do it If you want.
  You don't have to help me with my homework.
  Elsie doesn't have to get up early tomorrow.
- Question words go at the beginning of the question.
  How much homework do you have to do every day?
  When do we have to make a decision?

LANGUAGE PRACTICE

UNIT 8

can/can't, be allowed to

1 Write positive [+] or negative [–] sentences with *can* or *can't*.

1 Susanna / come with us tomorrow. [–]
   Susanna can't come with us tomorrow.

2 we / write in our English books. [+]
   _____

3 James / use his brother's bike. [+]
   _____

4 they / play in a professional orchestra. [–]
   _____

2 Write sentences with *be allowed to* and the verb in brackets.

1 We *'re allowed to wear* (wear) boots in the winter.
2 Andrea _____ (have) her laptop in class.
3 Franklin _____ (not /drive) his father's car.
4 Children _____ (not / be) rude to their parents.

3 Make questions and short answers with *be allowed to*.

1 your teachers / give detention / yes
   Are your teachers allowed to give detention?
   Yes, they are.

2 your little sister / wear make-up / no
   _____
   _____

3 they / use online dictionaries / yes
   _____
   _____

4 we / eat all these cakes / no
   _____
   _____

5 Carlos / play football with us / yes
   _____
   _____

have to, must and need to

4 Correct the mistake in each sentence.

1 She ~~don't~~ have to sit at the front of the class.
   She doesn't have to sit at the front of the class.

2 You have be well-behaved on the school bus.
   _____

3 Luis and his friend needs to finish their homework.
   _____

4 Must we to come into school at the weekend?
   _____

5 Circle the correct option.

1 It isn't necessary to write a thank-you letter.
   A (You don't have to write a letter.)   B You mustn't write a letter.

2 I can go to the gym by bike.
   A I need to take the bus.   B I don't need to take the bus.

3 It's important for me to revise for exams.
   A I don't need to revise.   B I must revise.

4 We're not allowed to run in the corridors.
   A We don't have to run, but we can.
   B We mustn't run.

5 You must watch this video!
   A I strongly recommend it.   B I don't think you'll like it.

6 Complete the swimming pool rules with the phrases in the box.

> don't have to use   don't need to bring
> have to have   have to wear   ~~mustn't come~~
> must remember   mustn't run   need to pay

You [1] *mustn't come* into the pool area in outdoor shoes. You [2] _____ rubber shoes round the pool. You [3] _____ attention on wet surfaces and you [4] _____ at any time. There are lockers in the changing rooms, but you [5] _____ them. You [6] _____ your own towel, because towels are provided. However, if you do use ours, you [7] _____ to leave them in the basket provided. Finally, swimmers under the age of ten [8] _____ an accompanying adult.

LANGUAGE REFERENCE & PRACTICE 103

LANGUAGE REFERENCE

UNIT 9

be going to and present continuous

Affirmative / Negative			Questions		
I	'm / 'm not	going to tell him.	Am I		going to tell him?
He / She / It	's / isn't		Is he / she / it		
We / You / They	're / aren't		Are we / you / they		

Short answers				
Yes,	I am.		No,	I'm not.
	he / she / it is.			he / she / it isn't.
	we / you / they are.			we / you / they aren't.

- We use **be going to** to talk about future actions we have decided to do.
  After we finish school, I'm going to travel to Australia.
  My grandparents are going to stay with us this summer.
- We use the appropriate present form of **be (not) + going + to + verb**.
  I'm going to wear my new jeans and my red T-shirt.
  We're not going to take the bus.
- We form questions with **be + subject + going + to + verb**.
  When are you going to start studying for the exams?
  Is she going to get here before 9 o'clock?

Present continuous for future

- We use the **present continuous** to talk about future arrangements when they have a fixed date.
  They're getting married this summer.
  What are you doing this weekend? I'm going shopping with my parents.

Future continuous

Affirmative / Negative		
I / You / He / She / It / We / You / They	will / won't may / may not might / might not	be lying on the beach this time next week.

Question			Short answers	
Will	I / you / he / she / it / we / you / they	be lying on the beach this time next week?	Yes, I / you / he / she / it / we / you / they will.	
			No, I / you / he / she / it / we / you / they won't.	

- We can use the **future continuous** to talk about actions in progress at a point in time in the future.
  My sister will be living in London next year. Next Saturday, we'll be sitting on the beach.
- We use **will/won't** when we feel sure about the action in progress, and **may (not)/might (not)** when we're less sure.
  They'll be answering questions online at 7 pm.
  We might be having dinner at 9 pm.

Relative pronouns and relative clauses

- We use **relative clauses** to make the person, place or thing we are talking about clear.
  My aunt has a friend who makes beautiful bags.
  This is the song that I told you about.
- We use **relative pronouns** at the beginning of relative clauses. We do not repeat the subject pronoun when the subject of the pronoun and following clause are the same.
  We know a lot of people who live in the village.
  ~~We know a lot of people who they live in the village.~~
- We use **who** or **that** to talk about people.
  The man who/that lives next door works at night.
  She's the scientist who's/that's moving to Antarctica next year.
- We use **that** or **which** to talk about things.
  I don't like books which/that have sad endings.
  I want boots which/that I can wear all year.
- We use **where** to talk about places.
  That's the office where my uncle works.
  Try the restaurant where we had my party.
- We use **when** to talk about time.
  That was the day when we were late for school.
  It's the holiday when everyone is happiest.
- We use **why** to talk about reasons.
  You studied a lot. That's why you passed!
  I lost my passport. That's why I'm so sad.
- We use **whose** to talk about possessions.
  Do you remember the name of the guy whose phone charger I borrowed last week?

LANGUAGE PRACTICE

UNIT 9

be going to and present continuous

1 Complete the sentences with the correct form of *be going to* and the verb in brackets.
1. We _are going to visit_ (visit) our old neighbours at the weekend.
2. She _____ (not come) with us to Peru.
3. He _____ (leave) for the station at nine.
4. They _____ (deliver) the products by drone next year.
5. Flights _____ (not be) cheaper in future, are they?
6. _____ you _____ (buy) the train tickets online?

Present continuous for future

2 Put the words in order.
1. train / travelling / on / to / the / night / Madrid / We're
   We're travelling to Madrid on the night train.
2. meeting / the / friends / their / They're / on / bus
   _____
3. on / summer / going / I'm / trip / this / school / a
   _____
4. for / you / Are / birthday / having / a / your / party / ?
   _____
5. tonight / isn't / our / Stella / to / concert / coming
   _____

Future continuous

3 Complete the text with the phrases in the box.

| will be building   will be cycling   ~~will be driving~~ |
| will be making   will be using   won't be doing |

More people ¹ _will be driving_ electric cars in the future, in my opinion. Transport companies ² _____ driverless trucks, too. But I wonder how teenagers ³ _____ their daily journeys in 20 years? Many believe that they ⁴ _____ more, but they ⁵ _____ that unless road conditions are improved. Today's keen cyclists hope that town planners ⁶ _____ more cycle lanes by the time their children are teenagers.

Relative pronouns and relative clauses

4 Circle the correct option.
1. I didn't know the person (who)/which sat next to me on the train.
2. She's the girl *who/whose* mother is from Chile.
3. Is August the time *which/when* it rains a lot in Scotland?
4. This is the book *that/whose* was banned in the 1940s.
5. That's the place *why/where* they used to meet.
6. It's the holidays and that's *where/why* I'm happy!

5 Correct the mistake in each sentence.
1. Do you know who bags these are?
   Do you know whose bags these are?
2. She can't remember when she wanted to buy.
   _____
3. That is the language school she will be studying.
   _____
4. I'll never forget the time which I met Adele.
   _____
5. Is there a reason where you don't want to fly?
   _____

6 Complete the conversation with the clauses in the box and the correct relative pronoun.

| father was the artist   told us   she recommended |
| was the artist   we could wait   ~~you took~~ |

ALEXIA Are those the photos ¹ _that/which you took_ on holiday?
KARL Yes, I took this one in Paris, remember?
ALEXIA Of course! It was our first day. We found a museum ² _____ for the rain to stop.
KARL That's right! And look – this was the girl ³ _____ about the exhibition.
ALEXIA Was she the person ⁴ _____?
KARL No, but she knew the man ⁵ _____ and that's ⁶ _____ the exhibition.

LANGUAGE REFERENCE & PRACTICE 105

LANGUAGE BANK

STARTER

Vocabulary
Technology

> app   device   emoji   screen
> social media   video chat

Feelings

> angry   bored   embarrassed
> excited   nervous   upset

Music

> bass   DJ   drums   fans   folk   heavy metal
> jazz   keyboard   rap   reggae

Language in action
Present simple and present continuous with adverbs of frequency
Present simple for future
Past simple

Writing
Useful language
… is a(n) … app
It's great because …
In my opinion, there are a couple of problems with it.
Overall, I think it's …
I really recommend it.

UNIT 1

Vocabulary
Describing people

> active   ambitious   calm   cheerful
> confident   helpful   inspiring   patient
> sensible   sensitive   sociable   talented

Phrasal verbs
cheer (somebody) up
deal with
depend on
get on with
give up
hang out
look up to
take care of

Language in action
Past simple and past continuous with *when*, *while* and *as*
Used to

Speaking
Everyday English
Go ahead.
Good for [her]!
I'm with you there.
The thing is …

Useful language
Can I ask you a few questions?
Can you tell us …?
First of all, …
One more thing …
That's all.

Writing
Useful language
For me, …
In my opinion, …
In my view, …
Personally, I think …

LANGUAGE BANK

UNIT 2

Vocabulary
Visual and performing arts

> architecture   contemporary dance   exhibition
> fashion design   filmmaking   gallery
> illustration   musical theatre   performance
> photography   sculpture   street art

Music and theatre

> audience   audition   lines   lyrics   orchestra
> part   rehearsal   scene   show   studio

Language in action
Present perfect with regular and irregular verbs
Present perfect with *already*, *just*, *still* and *yet*

Speaking
Everyday English
dunno
ginormous
kid
nope
tons

Useful language
It isn't supposed to …
It looks like …
It makes me feel …
It probably shows …
It seems a bit …

Writing
Useful language
Writing a review
I recommend it because …
I've never seen anything like it before.
It's on at …
It's the best show I've ever seen.
What I liked / didn't like about it was …

UNIT 3

Vocabulary
Communicating

> describe   gesture   greet   interpret
> post   shake hands   shout   smile
> translate   wave   whisper

Collocations with *say* and *tell*
Say: hello / (something) in Italian / sorry / yes/no
Tell: a joke / a lie / someone a secret / a story / the truth

Language in action
Can, could, will be able to
Present perfect with *for/since* and *How long …?*
Present perfect and past simple

Speaking
Everyday English
No worries.
Oh dear!
Phew!
Yep.

Useful language
I need them to …
It's a kind of …
They're similar to …
You use it to …

Writing
Useful language
Writing a listicle
all [his] life
before
later on
over the last few years
since
soon
these days

LANGUAGE BANK

UNIT 4

Vocabulary
Health and fitness

> cough   get better   get enough sleep   get ill
> get stressed   go jogging   have a fever   relax
> sneeze   sweat   train   warm up   work out

Healthy eating

> a balanced diet   calories   carbohydrates
> dairy products   fat   fibre   protein
> nutrition   vitamins

Language in action
Quantifiers
Should, *shouldn't* and *ought to*

Speaking
Everyday English
I'll give it a shot.
… isn't really my thing.
Seriously?
Tell me about it!

Useful language
How about … (+ *-ing*)?
Make sure you …
Something else I find useful …
… works for me.
You could just …

Writing
Useful language
Writing a post on a forum
Have you tried … (+ *-ing*)?
I recommend … (+ *-ing*)
That way, you can just …
Why don't you …?
You could always …

UNIT 5

Vocabulary
Planet Earth

> carbon dioxide   climate change
> endangered species   energy   marine life
> oxygen   pollution   solar power
> the environment   the planet   waste   wildlife

Natural environments

> bay   cave   cliff   coast   iceberg   stream
> rainforest   valley   volcano   waterfall

Language in action
The first conditional
The second conditional

Speaking
Everyday English
I'll give it a miss.
I'm off to …
It's not on.
Wanna join us?

Useful language
Don't forget that …
I see your point, but …
Let's agree to disagree.
Maybe you're right, but …
Remember that …

Writing
Useful language
Writing an opinion essay
Furthermore, …
However, …
In addition to this, …
In my opinion, …
In my view, …
Some people believe that, …
To sum up, …

LANGUAGE BANK

UNIT 6

Vocabulary
Making things

> add   boil   cover   dip   freeze
> increase   place   pour   press   pull
> reduce   remove   stir

Materials

> cardboard   glass
> leather   rubber   silk   tin

Containers

> bag   box   can
> case   jar   tube

Language in action
Present simple passive
Past simple passive

Speaking
Everyday English
any old …
Go for it!
Hang on a sec!
I get it.
kind of tricky

Useful language
Giving instructions
First of all, …
The next bit's …
Once (something is done), …
And there you have it!

Following instructions
Let me check I've got this right.
Oh, I see.
Then what?
What's next?

Writing
Useful language
Writing a review
However, I should point out that …
Overall, I think it is / they are …
The glasses look like …
The lenses are made from …
What I like about them is …

UNIT 7

Vocabulary
Festivals

> atmosphere   carnival   ceremon   costume
> crowd   decoration   firework   float
> funfair   lantern   parade   programme   stall

Music festivals and live music

> band member   campsite   encore
> gig   headliner   stage   support act
> tent   track   venue

Language in action
Past perfect
Reported statements

Speaking
Everyday English
at my place
Count me in.
It kicks off at …
I won't say a word.
The more the merrier.

Useful language
I'd love to.
I'll be there (at/around) …
Should I bring anything?
What are you up to …?
What time should I be there?

Writing
Useful language
Writing an email to a friend
Anyway, that's all from me.
Bye for now,
It was great to hear from you!
Thanks for your email.
Write back soon!

LANGUAGE BANK

UNIT 8

Vocabulary
School

> cheat in a test   fail an exam   get detention
> get good grades   hand in homework
> pass an exam   pay attention to the teacher
> revise for a test   take an exam
> tell somebody off   write an essay

Attitude and behaviour

> careful   careless   childish   disorganised
> mature   naughty   organised   polite
> rude   well-behaved

Language in action
Can/can't
Be allowed to
Have to, *must* and *need to*

Speaking
Everyday English
How come?
It's a lot to get your head around.
Kind of.
That's no big deal.
Yeah, right!

Useful language
Anything else I need to know?
What happens if you do?
What are the rules about …?
Why's that?

Writing
Useful language
Writing an essay
In this essay, I outline …
On the one hand, …
On the other hand, …
Others argue that …
Some say that …

UNIT 9

Vocabulary
Travel

> abroad   accommodation   backpacking
> booking   cruise ship   destination
> holiday resort   journey   sightseeing
> tour   tourist attraction   trip

Travel phrasal verbs

> check in   check out   get away   get back
> get in   go away   look around   set off   take off

Language in action
Be going to and present continuous for future
Future continuous
Relative pronouns and relative clauses

Speaking
Everyday English
… and so on.
bucket list
… right in the middle of …
stuff
What [were] you on about?

Useful language
How long are you going for?
I'm really looking forward to … (+ -*ing*)
… in two weeks' time.
We're going to try and …
What are you planning on doing?
Where will you be staying?

Writing
Useful language
Writing an email to a host family
Best wishes,
Dear Mr and Mrs …
Do you know …?
I'm writing to …
Thank you very much for … (+ -*ing*)

110 LANGUAGE BANK

IRREGULAR VERBS

Infinitive	Past simple	Past participle
be	was/were	been
beat	beat	beaten
become	became	become
begin	began	begun
bite	bit	bitten
blow	blew	blown
break	broke	broken
bring	brought	brought
build	built	built
buy	bought	bought
catch	caught	caught
choose	chose	chosen
come	came	come
cost	cost	cost
cut	cut	cut
do	did	done
draw	drew	drawn
drink	drank	drunk
drive	drove	driven
eat	ate	eaten
fall	fell	fallen
feel	felt	felt
fight	fought	fought
find	found	found
fly	flew	flown
forget	forgot	forgotten
get	got	got
give	gave	given
go	went	gone
grow	grew	grown
hang	hung	hung
have	had	had
hear	heard	heard
hide	hid	hidden
hit	hit	hit
hold	held	held
hurt	hurt	hurt
keep	kept	kept
know	knew	known
leave	left	left
lend	lent	lent
let	let	let
lie	lied	lied
light	lit	lit
lose	lost	lost
make	made	made
mean	meant	meant
meet	met	met
pay	paid	paid
put	put	put
read	read	read
ride	rode	ridden
ring	rang	rung
rise	rose	risen
run	ran	run
say	said	said
see	saw	seen
sell	sold	sold
send	sent	sent
shine	shone	shone
shoot	shot	shot
show	showed	shown
shut	shut	shut
sing	sang	sung
sit	sat	sat
sleep	slept	slept
speak	spoke	spoken
spend	spent	spent
stand	stood	stood
steal	stole	stolen
swim	swam	swum
take	took	taken
teach	taught	taught
tear	tore	torn
tell	told	told
think	thought	thought
throw	threw	thrown
understand	understood	understood
wake	woke	woken
wear	wore	worn
win	won	won
write	wrote	written

Acknowledgements

The authors and publishers acknowledge the following sources of copyright material and are grateful for the permissions granted. While every effort has been made, it has not always been possible to identify the sources of all the material used, or to trace all copyright holders. If any omissions are brought to our notice, we will be happy to include the appropriate acknowledgements on reprinting & in the next update to the digital edition, as applicable.

Key: SU= Starter Unit; U = Unit.

Text

U1: Text about Derek Rabelo. Copyright © Derek Rabelo. Reproduce with permission; U2: Text about Lorenzo Quinn. Copyright © Lorenzo Quinn. Reproduced with kind permission; Text about Alma Deutscher. Copyright © Alma Deutscher. Reproduced with kind permission of Guy Deutscher.

Photography

The following photographs are sourced from Getty Images.

SU: Monkey Business Images/Getty Images Plus; Viktor Holm/Folio; Sidekick/E+; relato/iStock/Getty Images Plus; Pekic/E+; Mima Foto/EyeEm; tuulijumala/iStock/Getty Images Plus; Dmytro Synelnychenko/iStock/Getty Images Plus; PT Images; Westend61; **U1:** GRANT ELLIS/AFP; Klisarova/Moment; Ryan McVay/Photodisc; Ulrik Tofte/Photodisc; Nenov/iStock/Getty Images Plus; Jupiterimages/Stockbyte; Morsa Images/DigitalVision; Compassionate Eye Foundation/Jetta Productions/Stockbyte; Lawrence Manning/Corbis; Klaus Vedfelt/DigitalVision; fizkes/iStock/Getty Images Plus; Digital Vision; **U2:** David_Ahn/iStock/Getty Images Plus; JOE KLAMAR/AFP; KidStock/Blend Images; Daria Botieva/Eyeem; ollo/iStock Unreleased; Kathrin Ziegler/DigitalVision; starman72/RooM; Zero Creatives/Cultura; kpalimski/iStock/Getty Images Plus; Brian Caissie; Adam Berry/Getty Images News; Vagengeym_Elena/iStock/Getty Images Plus; Vit_Mar/iStock/Getty Images Plus; Mike Harrington/DigitalVision; Hero Images; fStop Images - Holger Hill/Brand X Pictures; Foodcollection RF; Ryan McVay/Photodisc; Tetra Images; miodrag ignjatovic/E+; d1sk/iStock/Getty Images Plus; Fuse/Corbis; **U3:** MikeCherim/E+; Westend61; praetorianphoto/E+; Tetra Images; Juanmonino/iStock/Getty Images Plus; Blend Images - KidStock/Brand X Pictures; Rene Frederick/Photodisc; recep-bg/E+; hkuchera/iStock/Getty Images Plus; Erik Isakson/Blend Images; Jose Luis Pelaez Inc/Blend Images; **U4:** Stanislaw Pytel/DigitalVision; SCIEPRO/Science Photo Library; Jose Luis Pelaez Inc/DigitalVision; gbh007/iStock/Getty Images Plus; monkeybusinessimages/iStock/Getty Images Plus; Hero Images; Dmytro Synelnychenko/iStock/Getty Images Plus; NYS444/iStock/Getty Images Plus; Cavan Images; Hill Street Studios/Blend Images; pixelpot/iStock/Getty Images Plus; Lemanieh/iStock/Getty Images Plus; margouillatphotos/iStock/Getty Images Plus; Ross Woodhall/Cultura; monticelllo/iStock/Getty Images Plus; filmfoto/iStock/Getty Images Plus; RascalRJ/Moment Open; ShowVectorStudio/iStock/Getty Images Plus; VikiVector/iStock/Getty Images Plus; apixel/E+; GMint/iStock/Getty Images Plus; Tetra Images; anouchka/iStock/Getty Images Plus; Vasily Pindyurin; Image Source; Muriel de Seze/DigitalVision; asiseeit/E+; mihailomilovanovic/E+; **U5:** Steve Clancy Photography/Moment; Peter Dazeley/Photographer's Choice RF; FotoDuets/iStock/Getty Images Plus; Thanatham Piriyakarnjanakul/EyeEm; Herianus Herianus/EyeEm; pepifoto/E+; Westend61; AlinaYudina/iStock/Getty Images Plus; paul mansfield photography/Moment; Sebastián Crespo Photography/Moment; Photos by R A Kearton/Moment Open; Timothy Mbugua/EyeEm; zhuzhu/iStock/Getty Images Plus; JLR/Moment; Ippei Naoi/Moment; Milton Cogheil/EyeEm; Yevgen Timashov/Cultura; Paola Moschitto-Assenmacher/EyeEm; Matteo Colombo/Moment; Marko Konig; Ricardo Funari/Brazil Photos/LightRocket; Matt Cardy/Getty Images News; GREG BAKER/AFP; SeaTops; **U6:** Food Delight/EyeEm; mm88/iStock/Getty Images Plus; Monty Rakusen/Cultura; Photographer is my life./Moment; stevanovicigor/iStock/Getty Images Plus; Kiran Ridley/Barcroft Images/Barcroft Media; hocus-focus/iStock Unreleased; Poh Kim Yeoh/EyeEm; flyfloor/E+; **U7:** Keren Su/China Span; John W Banagan/Photographer's Choice; FernandoQuevedo/iStock Editorial/Getty Images Plus; merc67/iStock Editorial/Getty Images Plus; Alexander W Helin/Moment; © Philippe LEJEANVRE/Moment; Oscar G Davila/EyeEm; Andreas Rentz/Getty Images Entertainment; pxel66/iStock/Getty Images Plus; Satoshi-K/iStock Unreleased; nevereverro/iStock Unreleased; gavran333/iStock/Getty Images Plus; 101cats/E+; Bettmann; Matthew Eisman/Redferns; Hero Images; Aleksandr_Vorobev/iStock Editorial/Getty Images Plus; olmozott98/iStock Editorial/Getty Images Plus; BILL WECHTER/AFP Contributor; Kevin Winter/Getty Images Entertainment; SAKhanPhotography/iStock/Getty Images Plus; **U8:** Juice Images; Lafforgue/Art In All Of Us/Corbis News; Hero Images; mushakesa/iStock/Getty Images Plus; piola666/E+; Wavebreakmedia/iStock/Getty Images Plus; Hero Images; TadejZupancic/E+; skynesher/E+; **U9:** Marka/Universal Images Group; arturbo/iStock/Getty Images Plus; iLexx/iStock/Getty Images Plus; PhonlamaiPhoto/iStock/Getty Images Plus; andruxevich/iStock/Getty Images Plus; inhauscreative/E+; Ed Freeman/The Image Bank/Getty Images Plus; Peter Samuels/DigitalVision; matthewleesdixon/iStock/Getty Images Plus; balipadma/iStock/Getty Images Plus.

The following photographs are sourced from another library.

U1: Copyright © Derek Rabelo; **U2:** Courtesy of the artist Lorenzo Quinn.

Illustration

U3: Amber Day; **U4:** Joanna Kerr; **U7:** Oliver Flores; **U9:** Joanna Kerr.

Typesetting: Blooberry Design

Cover illustration: Collaborate Agency

Audio recordings: Creative Listening

Video production: Lucentum Digital

Freelance editing: Jacqueline French, Matthew Duffy, Nicola Foufouti